Dedicated to Rob Edwards 1984-2018

Agencynomics

Agency and Economics. It's that simple.

We coined the phrase Agencynomics after many years of running and advising Agencies. When coming up against competitive Agencies, in pitches or at social events, we would hear them quoting the most incredible numbers and statistics to back up their performance.

Time and again we'd be left scratching our heads in wonder, asking, "How can a competitor from a business similar to ours achieve such incredible results or such high profits?"

Over time we started to uncover the truth; typically we would discover these competitors had disclosed their best sales month ever, multiplied that by 12 and added taxes.

Sure, it's good to talk up your business sometimes, most of us do. But the problem is, misinformation is often damaging. It certainly was for us, because after hearing these figures we'd often believe them and return to our business a little depressed. What we needed was a more truthful benchmark.

Over the years we learnt that by meeting at least three complementary businesses, we could build a more accurate picture of how our competitors were actually performing; or at least gather a range of truths.

We started to learn the right questions to ask people so that we could distinguish the honest ones from those who exaggerated or over-spun.

What we came to realise was, underneath the bonnet, a lot of Agency businesses share many common characteristics in the way they are structured.

So now let us share with you the underlying facts and figures of Agencies so that you can benchmark yourself more accurately.

We even coined our own term, Agencynomics, to describe the mechanics of just how a traditional Agency business works; everything from the key metrics, to the KPIs and the essential structures which Agencies are built on.

We liked the phrase Agencynomics so much that we trademarked it and have now named our book after it. We hope you enjoy reading and use it to enable your Agency to grow and succeed!

Spencer and Pete

Our Story

It all began in 1999 when I, Spencer Gallagher, started K2 Consulting, which incorporated in 2001 as Bluhalo Limited. After a few years, I was joined by Peter Hoole who became Finance Director (FD) in 2004.

During those next few years between 2004 and 2008, the Agency grew a staggering 1100%, appearing almost annually during that period in the Deloitte Tech Fast 50 and EMEA Fast 500, and in many other league tables too.

In 2007 we worked on preparing Bluhalo for sale with BDO Stoy Hayward, one of the world's largest accountancy firms. The company was successfully sold to Gyro International, the world's largest independent B2B marketing Agency in April 2008. Gyro was then acquired by the Dentsu Aegis Network in 2016.

The acquisition helped Bluhalo access Gyro's offices globally, enabling Bluhalo to design, build and market some of the world's largest websites. The newly merged entity, trading as Bluhalo/Gyro, became a top 10 UK digital marketing Agency, recognised by the New Media Age league table both in 2009 and 2010.

While I, Spencer, was busy running the digital business, and having a role in Gyro's leadership team, I, Pete, took on the additional responsibility of becoming Finance Director for two other Gyro owned businesses, Woolley Pau and Woolley Pau PR, in addition to remaining Finance Director for Bluhalo.

In 2011 we co-founded Cactus to help fast growing and ambitious Agencies successfully accelerate their business goals and objectives.

This new consultancy provided Agency clients with expert commercial development support, combined with operational and specialist Agency financial guidance.

Cactus Agencies are now some of the fastest growing in Europe and are consistently recognised in industry league tables and awards for their high standard of work and fast growth.

In 2013, shortly after we formed Cactus to provide consultancy to support Agencies looking to scale.

We started to receive calls almost daily from Agencies who were either struggling to survive or struggling to grow.

At the time there was little support for Agency founders, many of whom didn't have a business partner to talk to.

In 2018 we wrote Agencynomics and in 2020, during the Covid-19 period, we launched our free community which is the largest, free of charge, UK community for Agency Founders.

Our mission now is to provide first class consultancy, training, expert knowledge and ethically sourced data to help the next generation of Agency people scale their Agency businesses.

Today we also speak at a wide range of events, both public, and within companies such as Google, on the subject of the business and future of Agencies.

This book couldn't have happened with a lot of help from a lot of people.

We would like to take this opportunity to say thank you to Bryony Waite, Melanie Nabarro, Jazz Thompson, Susanna Simpson, Jacqueline Burns, Lesley Gallagher, Lucy Hoole, Kelly Molson, Nathan Lomax, Jodie Simpson, Lee Nathan, Vicki Vinton, Joe Rice, Prisca Moyesa and Ruby Marquet-Horwood.

We would also like to give a special mention to Mark Probert who works with us at Cactus, running our Scottish Division.

Mark technically could be called the third author of book with the amount of time, support and contributions he has made to help us finish this book.

CONTENTS

Chapter 1: Intro

Six years later
Different strokes
Under the bonnet
You in or out?

Chapter 2: Let's Get Started

Easy peasy
In the beginning
Manifesto
Lifestyle v scalable
Location, location, location
One vision
Meet beat
Focus, focus, focus

Chapter 3: Money, Money, Money

Fifteen minute finance
Meet the banker
Not so board meetings
Having a plan
Monthly reporting
Milestones
Growing through the numbers
Rate Setting
EBIT-DUH?

Chapter 4: Sales & Marketing 101

Sales is a dirty word
One billion pounds
The one percent
To pitch or not to pitch
Chemistry & creds
Mind mapping
Frenemies & more
When will I be famous?
Competitive intelligence
#FFFF
Thinking & doing

Chapter 5: Delivering Happiness

Parkinson's law
The PM
Don't go chasing waterfalls
Psychometrics
What's in it for me? (WIIFM)
Process workflow
Visualising process
Alignment
Great expectations
Under promise, over deliver
Day rates
Working styles

Chapter 6: Agency Tribal Structures

4-4-2 or 5-3-2?
Pyramids & pods
ABR principle
People are your only asset
Unravelling spaghetti
The holy grail
A new world order

Chapter 7: Agency Anthropology

Happy team, happy client
Work, rest and duvet days
Cornerstones
Talent scout
Wood for the trees

Chapter 8: Outro

Concluding thoughts

Chapter 9: The Agencynomics

Agency metrics, an intro
Benchmarking

Chapter 10: All Leaders are Readers

Recommended reading

Bonus Section: Agencynomics Tips

Sales, marketing & account management
Financial intelligence
Leadership culture and talent
Service delivery

Chapter 1: Intro

SIX YEARS LATER

We started writing this book in 2012. Having written 80% of it, our business growth took over and we put the book to one side.

It's now six years later, and as we write this section we are pleased we waited. The high-level experience we have gained since putting our book to one side, has increased our knowledge tenfold.

We are happy to share what we have learnt from working in the business at every level: from building a business in a back garden shed, to running a £12m Agency and working as part of the leadership team in a £100m one.

Today, we now run Cactus, the UK's leading Agency growth consultancy, we have spoken to over 3,000 Agencies worldwide and helped over 1,000 Agencies directly since its formation in 2011.

We always say that we learnt 25% of this job by having been there and done it, and we continue to gain new first hand understanding on how Agency growth works. But the extra 75% of our knowledge has come from our contact and work with over 1,000 Agencies since we sold Bluhalo.

Initially this book was designed to be read by so-called 'digital' Agencies, because in 2012 they were very much at the heart of the Advertising and Marketing transformation taking place.

Six years later, the distinction between digital and ordinary Agencies no longer applies. This is because in today's world, 99% of Agencies simply would not exist without digital channels. Consequently, this book is now aimed at all creative, innovative and marketing type Agencies.

Now we share our strategies with Agencies who, over the past six years, have grown an average of 80% each year. We've learnt why it is that some Agencies scale slower and some faster.

In this book we share with you our own Agency strategies as well as the strategies of Agencies – large and small - who do things the right way.

This book isn't a blow-by-blow instruction manual, instead it is designed to help you sanely check the things you are doing well and enable you to identify new strategies to build extra momentum.

Equally, it's a not a "System" or "Playbook" with a secret range of courses designed to "lock you in" post or during reading this book.

We've also added 100 practical tips, ideas and metrics in our Bonus Section at the back of book.

Chapter Two will be of particular use to you if you are at the very beginning of your journey or planning to start out. We suggest to those of you already well on the way to start at Chapter Three. Feel free to choose between reading the book cover to cover, or to just cherry pick those sections which feel most relevant to you.

As comprehensive as this book is, there are others that cover specific subjects in greater depth, consequently in Chapter Ten we've included a recommended reading list.

In the future, we also intend to share additional useful tools and documents with our followers, via our website and social media, so please keep checking back in.

This book will answer your questions on how to scale an Agency and provide you with some industry metrics to help you benchmark your current performance. We've done the hard work and we think we've got the answers and we are happy to give away information here that usually we are paid to do.

But we want to make it absolutely clear that the single most important factor which separates an Agency success from failure, is its willingness to embrace and adopt a growth mindset.

Lastly, while this book has been written using £GBP, our work with Agencies from all over the world has demonstrated that our advice is borderless.

DIFFERENT STROKES

The primary task of an Agency is to help solve the problems that are presented to it, by its clients.

Clients ask Agencies to do this as they usually don't have the knowledge, skills, time or resources to solve those problems themselves.

This might sound obvious but one of the things that Agencies often forget is why their Agency exists.

Always remain focused on how you can help organisations and focus on the outcomes and results they want, or the problems they need fixing, rather than just communicating a list of services your Agency can deliver.

Whether you are a creative, innovative, technical or marketing Agency, your business model and structure will be essentially similar, with only the subtlest of variances. The majority of your billings will be through the sale of services based on time or value, rather than through the sale of tangible goods or products.

This book will be of most use to any creative, design, brand, marketing, advertising, technology or digital Agencies.

It will be less relevant to media sales or recruitment Agencies; and while we cover strategic consultancy as an Agency service, we would class pure consultancies as outside the scope of this book. PR businesses often have a hybrid model compared to traditional Agencies, although with the convergence of 'influencer' and social media/content services, they are becoming increasingly more aligned with this book's approach.

That said, even if you are a service business, we are sure that you will still pick up some gems from this book. For example, if you work as a lawyer or accountant, we would ask you to test out the 30/30/30/10 inbound lead generation method, outlined further on.

UNDER THE BONNET

Let's be clear from the outset; our intention is not to answer your client's briefs, help you deliver ideas, create an award-winning creative campaign or help you innovate a new product or service for a client!

This book will assume that you and your team are already wonderfully talented and fabulously spectacular at providing the best services you offer.

We are not intending this book to be a fix-all for all your business challenges, nor is it designed as a step by step handbook.

YOU IN, OR OUT?

This book is for anyone who is:

- Thinking of starting an Agency, running an Agency, or wants to grow an Agency.

- Freelancers who want to know how to scale from one to two or more people.

- A one to five person Agency owner or Director aspiring to get to your first £1m turnover with 15 to 16 staff.

- An Agency owner or Director, who may be just under or over the £1m in fees (or gross profit level), and is looking to grow from 10 to 20, 30, 40 or 50 people.

- Medium sized Agency owners and Directors with aspirations of owning a 50 person, £5m business with 20% net profit.

- More substantial Agencies, who will most likely know most of the details of this book yet are looking for any extra nuggets of information which they may have overlooked, or who are seeking validation of their Agency growth techniques.

That said, when we recently did a talk on lead generation for Agencies, the person who was seen to write the most notes was the Founder of the largest Agency in the room. At the end of the talk he came up to us and said, "We used to do all these things, but have lost our way lately, so thank you for the reminder".

This book is not for people who:

- Aren't serious about growing their Agency.

- Don't want ideas on how to improve their business.

- Have a fixed mindset.

Chapter 2: Let's Get Started

EASY PEASY

We think that starting an Agency is possibly one of the most straightforward businesses to embark upon.

Let us begin by saying that anyone can set up an Agency. Yes, anyone. There are very few barriers to developing your own Agency business.

Typically, there are two types of Agency founder. The first is the individual who has either already worked within the Agency space, or is a freelancer working within the Agency or client sector. The second is the person who comes from a commercial or entrepreneurial background and has seen an opportunity within this sector.

In more recent years, we have also noticed a significant trend of people starting Agencies straight out of college or university.

Whether you are someone with a skill you plan to offer as a service, or an Entrepreneur looking to sell a service, you will find this following section helpful in getting you started, and a useful guide through those early stages.

IN THE BEGINNING

Probably the best way for us to explain the beginnings of an Agency is to start with Spencer's first-hand story of starting out, and then offer our combined thoughts on our experiences of meeting lots of people who were either looking to start an Agency, or who had just started out.

Spencer's story

In 1998 after having three jobs in one year and being made redundant from two of them, I read a book called What Colour is Your Parachute? by Richard Nelson Bolles. I think the illustration below visualises really clearly what this book made me realise.

★ *PURPOSE*

My life purpose became more evident for the first time when I joined the dots and looked back at my career as a whole. I left school, was always playing with computers in my spare time, and building websites was a real passion for me so my personal interests and work interests collided. It was like everything was leading to the point where at age of 27, I started my own business. I had always known I'd have my own business one day, but a redundancy forced me into going it alone and I'm grateful for it.

With only £4,500 to my name (my last pay cheque), I worked out that I could survive for three months at £1,500 a month. I figured that if I could sell enough websites by the fourth month then I would have a business.

Many people I know take this route. They have some money saved up, start a business, and force themselves to achieve a goal to succeed before the money runs out, usually within a year. In my case, three months may have been a little optimistic. The essential learning for me here was unquestionably the importance of setting deadlines and targets for success from the outset, albeit in a small way to begin with.

I also had to learn when to cut my losses. There is a fine line between persistence based on a firm belief, and a relentless positivity which blinds you from recognising the things that you will never make work.

Like many people who start an Agency, I had very little Agency exposure or experience. With a sales background in retail, I was more of an entrepreneurial venturer than a seasoned Agency executive starting out.

Despite this, I had a passion for technology gained from discovering the internet in the early 90's and believed I could sell anything I was passionate about. I saw a market opportunity coming in the form of an increasing demand for websites and new media services - as we affectionately called them back then.

It was around this time that I heard a story about a UK Building Society paying £80,000 for a 12-page website and I thought, perhaps naively; "I could do that for a few thousand, just give me one of those deals a month, I'd have a business!".

I later learnt that almost half the people starting an Agency, like me had no real Agency experience. In fact, for three years I didn't even know that I was running an Agency....I thought I was a tech business!

Business owners can feel under constant pressure in the early days. It is hard to come away from each day not feeling defeated and so it is vital to have support.

I've seen far too many people impart their fears of failure onto their Agency owning partners, which can make them doubt their ability to succeed.

Knowing this, a key task was to get the support of my girlfriend who ran two successful branches of her own business. I knew that I was taking a risk; potentially in three months time I'd be without a salary.

She warned me that it would be hard, asked me if I was sure I wanted to do this, and then gave me her blessing, in a 'this is going to be harder than you think' way.

My journey could begin in the knowledge that I had the support of those around me. I knew I was going to need it and I was right, that support was critical to my success.

Recently I met a wonderfully enthused Agency owner. His business is rapidly growing, and he told me a story about his own partner, who had a 'growth mindset'. She had shared her philosophy with him, and whenever he had doubts, his partner was there to bring him right back.

Good support is like gold dust so do seek that support out for yourself. Unsurprisingly that girlfriend of mine became my wife.

Another key task was to find a business name; funny how something so simple is often so hard.

Inspiration came during a long-standing snowboarding trip (which was just one week away from when I'd planned to start my business).

I was at the top of a mountain, sitting admiring the view and worrying that I was running out of time to find a name for my business, when I saw a fellow snowboarder (and you need to know that we were a rare breed back in 1999). As he turned his board around I noticed it had K2 written across it, with an image of the mountain. Bingo!

For those who unlike me have more of a marketing or branding background, there are much more structured ways to create your brand identity.

If you have the time and money then yes, invest in proper strategy and branding, and by all means get trademarks done, but don't let it slow down the formation of your business. For me the investment in getting my branding right came later. At the beginning as a small start-up, with limited funds, finding inspiration on a snowboard was my only route.

Though it's not just the cash cost of a branding strategy, it's the time investment too. Be aware that it can take months, despite most people's optimistic timescales. In my experience, it typically takes our clients today six-12 months to get branding done properly.

Next, I needed an office. I was living just outside London, without a car following my redundancy, when fortunately, my late mother, who lived nearby, offered me the large purple shed in her garden as office space. This arrangement meant that I could keep my costs low, allowing me to further bootstrap my new start-up.

Today, with all the flexible and co-op working spaces available, and remote working more standard, there are more alternatives than ever to the classic, garage, shed or dining room table.

In the early stage of an Agency, the costs of a decent office can outstrip the benefits. That said, the right office in the right location just may attract the sales and new business you need.

But you are warned, the overall strategy for success is to find the sales first, then invest in people and offices, not the other way around.

The next step was to register a company and I opted for sole trader status. People I'd met along the way had advised me that this would be a better route to choose because the likely risk to a financial loss was low. With hindsight, I now understand that this is not necessarily the case. In fact, I should have consulted with an accountant regarding the formation of the business and its legal structure.

But these days if you want to register a limited business, it's easier than ever to do it online. A friendly local accountant will always provide some initial free advice on the route you ought to take. Just make sure that you ask for two or three opinions first.

I then went to the bank as I needed a business account. The bank wanted a business-plan in the application, which I cobbled together, and they introduced me to a local business consultant. More about that in the section on Non-execs and other external advisors. It's worth saying two things about how to select the right bank for your business.

Firstly, it's less about the brand you choose, and more about the person who will be managing your accounts. Try and get a recommendation for a good bank manager from a few people you know.

However the second point we'd like to make is that we are increasingly likely to see challenger banks disrupting the business and commercial banking space. This will make the account opening process simpler, but may eventually make the traditional bank manager redundant, thereby rendering meaningless the advice above about finding the right bank manager!

In my case the key factor was that I didn't want to borrow money, which made the application simpler.

Now that I was armed with a company name, business account and a self-made logo, I needed to get business cards and stationery (nowadays perhaps less critical acquisitions). Using Microsoft Office, it was easy to invoice. But these days a subscription to an accounting package like Xero will help tremendously, in the early stages, with the invoicing and processing of receipts. Compared to their predecessors, they are much easier for business owners to use.

My (Spencer) Agency consisted of just me in the beginning; no business partners. We often get asked about this, and the truth is that the more partners there are at the beginning, the bigger the financial overhead. When the business becomes larger, having more partners can be helpful, especially if their skill sets are different. On the other hand, the more business partners there are, the more likely they are to fall-out with one another at some point in the journey. So, if you are starting out with business partners from day one, then the right advice would be to get a shareholders agreement in place. The reality is that drawing up an agreement of this nature is quite cost prohibitive when the business is in start-up phase. So at least sit down with your partners and agree how you would deal with a fall-out in the future, and then document it together.

If you are the one and only owner, it can be quite lonely at times. You may miss the support of others, but you'll often find the decision-making process is much quicker than if there were partners involved. It's a trade-off.

If there are two, three or four of you, the most important thing to make sure of is that your skill sets are complementary. Whether those skills be sales, client account/strategy management, project management, business processes/ operations, creative, technical, or finance; the less overlay the better.

I have also noticed either being (or having) a more extroverted client/sales focused partner, or number two, can be vital.

On the eve of the third month in business, I took my soon-to-be-wife out to dinner (or rather being more successful, she took me). I had only just hit the £1,500 target I needed for month four and that had taken me three months to achieve! It's worth noting that I had also taken on part-time cleaning jobs at £100 a day to help towards reaching that target and continue the business. We both agreed that I was going to struggle in four more weeks to find another £1,500 to survive into month five.

I went to my office the next day to shut down K2 and go back to getting a normal job, but as I walked into my shed office, the phone rang. It was a client with confirmation of an order for a £5,000 website, suddenly I had four more months of income!

And the business had begun!

My (Spencer) first-year sales as an Agency were only £30,000, but that was ok. Yes, it should have been £50,000, which was my previous year's salary, but I was realistic about the minimum I needed to survive and keep my business trading.

So, there we have it. As you can see it's relatively simple to start an Agency, getting it off the ground is another story!

MANIFESTO

Once I had found my purpose, the important thing now was to make sure that my services were aligned. This positioning would change a few times over the years as K2 scaled into Blue Halo Media, and then finally Bluhalo.

Initially, I was planning to sell websites to anyone who wanted one. I had heard many stories of Agencies' extortionate pricing, whereas I intended that my pricing would be authentic, helping small businesses get online, rather than taking advantage of them. This was my purpose and it is essential that you keep verbally communicating your purpose to your team (when you have one) on a weekly basis. This way you will be validating all the steps that you are taking towards achieving your goals.

In my opinion, the most important thing is to start by visualising the journey you intend to take. In my own Agency's journey, the positioning and focusing work came much later, at around the £1m and once again at the £2m turnover level. I've seen this to be the same case for many others too; the reason being that when you start off you may not yet know where to focus. It takes time to find the market sweet spot that you want to engage with, it's not something that can be forced.

While I am going to cover your journey at a high level for you, I would also urge you at some stage to get outside help. I worked with James Henderson of Brilliant Path located in London, UK for many years, as he is a specialist in Agency positioning. Find someone who not only understands brand, but also has a solid understanding of the Agency space and your target markets.

Today, in our consulting role, it's imperative that we keep reminding the Agencies we work with that there is a now, next and future to their service proposition. Your service proposition must keep slowly evolving away from being commoditised, and it is important not to risk the service being potentially taken back in-house by your clients.

The following illustration should help explain this.

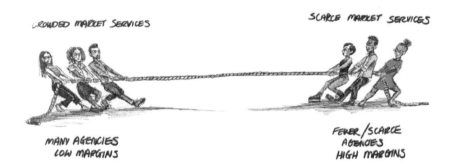

CROWDED MARKET SERVICES

SCARCE MARKET SERVICES

MANY AGENCIES
LOW MARGINS

FEWER /SCARCE
AGENCIES
HIGH MARGINS

There is also a decision for you to make on how focused your Agency is with your branding and proposition. There is an old saying that goes along the line of "the narrower the focus the deeper you cut" which the illustration below demonstrates.

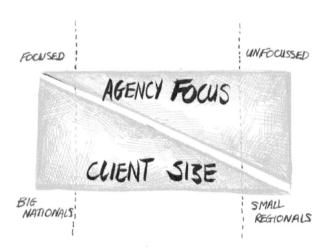

Mission statement

A mission statement is a short statement of an organisation's purpose, identifying the scope of its operations. It should include a description of what kind of product or service it provides, its primary customers or market and its geographical region of operation.

Here are some good examples of mission statements:

Patagonia: "Build the best product, cause no unnecessary harm, use business to inspire and implement solutions to the environmental crisis."

Amazon: "We seek to be Earth's most customer-centric company for four primary customer sets: consumers, sellers, enterprises, and content creators."

Tesla: "To accelerate the advent of sustainable transport by bringing compelling mass market electric cars to market as soon as possible."

Leo Burnett Worldwide: "We create ideas that inspire enduring belief."

WPP: "To develop and manage talent; to apply that talent, throughout the world, for the benefit of clients; to do so in partnership; to do so with profit."

Vision statement

The vision statement defines the optimal desired future state, the mental picture of what an organisation wants to achieve over time. It provides guidance and inspiration, by explaining what an organisation is focussed on achieving over three, five, ten, or more years.

The vision of Zappos.com is "Delivering happiness to customers, employees, and vendors."

Oxfam: "A just world without poverty"

Ustwo: "Our vision is to create a world where digital experiences transform people's daily lives."

Kiva: "We envision a world where all people – even in the most remote areas of the globe – hold power to create an opportunity for themselves and others."

Creative Commons: "Nothing less than realising the full potential of the internet — universal access to research and education, full participation in culture — to drive a new era of development, growth, and productivity."

The difference between mission and vision:

A mission statement defines the company's business, its objectives and its approach to reaching those objectives.

A vision statement describes the desired future position of the company. Elements of mission and vision statements are often combined to provide a statement of the company's purposes, goals and values.

Value statement

A value statement is a declaration which informs the customers, and the staff of a business, what the firm's top priorities and core beliefs are.

A company often uses a value statement to help it identify and connect with targeted consumers, as well as to remind its employees about their priorities and goals.

We were always inspired by Zappos CEO Tony Hsieh's book, *Delivering Happiness.* However, much Zappos have evolved their innovative approach to managing their business, their approach to core values has always remained intact.

LIFESTYLE VS SCALABLE

There are two types of motives for running a business: to create the lifestyle you want or to build a large company, something that scales.

The route you choose comes down to your **VISION**.

Your route and vision can change. Initially Spencer was happy just to get to an Agency of eight people, but at eight people he decided he wanted to scale and build something bigger.

A lifestyle business is, yes you guessed it, set up to suit a lifestyle. It's an Agency setup, run by its founders with the aim of sustaining a particular level of income and no more; or it is designed to provide a foundation for a particular lifestyle to be enjoyed.

There is no real need to employ anyone within a lifestyle organisation, but many do have a core team, typically of two to 10 people, although it could run to as many as 20. You can use freelancers and a handful of team members, who are also lifestyle driven, but these companies tend to have no grand ambitions to scale. This style of business makes up the majority of Agencies.

It is reported that 250,000 freelancers and Agencies in the UK have less than five staff. It is a fun, less stressful, and potentially more lucrative way to run your business, and you can say no to opportunities. But your business is often not structured, which means that when you retire, or have finally had enough, you will usually be its only value, and the company will be sold for goodwill, if at all.

A scalable business is one whose vision is to grow into a much larger company. These Agencies tend to have ambitious and tenacious leaders, who are prepared to recruit, are continually driven to win larger clients and will make sacrifices and take the calculated risks to get there.

They are the 'yes people' of business, always taking on the right sort of activity to expand their company, even if it affects their social life. This form of activity often requires sacrifices in the early stages, as the owners may at times have to pay their employees before they pay themselves. However, their perseverance means that one day the scalable business can be sold or support them through retirement; perhaps even early retirement.

When we first started Cactus, we were inundated with calls from people in their 50's and 60's looking to sell their lifestyle Agencies so they could retire.

These owners were all surprised how little their sub £1m turnover Agencies were actually worth.

They had spent the past 10 to 20 years building their lifestyle Agency, drawing all the profits out of the business but not reinvesting.

Our message to you is, please know what you are trying to achieve. The chances of selling and exiting an Agency we estimate to be as low as 0.25%, that's a 1 in 400 chance of selling your business.

You need to decide if you want a 'lifestyle' business, one where you take a living wage and use it to invest in your eventual retirement. Or are you scaling the Agency so at some stage in the future, should you decide to, you can sell the Agency for a sizable sum to profit from all your hard work?

There is no right or wrong answer here, it's a highly personal choice for you to make on your approach.

Some founders want to scale, but never want to sell, they just want to build an Agency that will last and create a legacy. If you decide to scale up and exit one day that's great, but be clear on how you intend to grow value in your business, and what you want your end-game to be. Then you can forget about it and get on with building an exceptional, best in class Agency.

As people who had scaled and exited, we were initially quite anti-lifestyle businesses. Indeed, Spencer had seen both his parents with lifestyle businesses end up with very little to show post retiring. But although the lifestyle option didn't seem to make sense to us at the time, we have softened our perspective on it now. However, we would still urge you to have a solid financial strategy and life plan. Stash away for your retirement; take out financial investments elsewhere, including pension plans; aim to pay your mortgage off; and seek to save 27 times what you need to live off as a total sum post mortgage.

E.g. with no mortgage you need £5k a month for expenses when retired, which means you'll need £1.62m (60k annually x 27) saved to retire fully.

Create the investments you'll need to get you there. Don't worry too much though - you've probably got 20 years to plan for that, and by that stage the world will be run by Artificial Intelligence and robots, we will 3D print everything and need far less money to survive on!

LOCATION, LOCATION, LOCATION

It's a big advantage to base yourself in a major city rather than a provincial area. Though we didn't start out that way: Bluhalo started its Agency journey in an old barn conversion on a farm in the countryside. Once we'd grown to about 40 people, we moved to some ultra modern offices located in a larger town just 30 minutes from London (8.8 million population), with excellent transport links to other major cities. We now had the access to talent, transport and clients we lacked earlier.

There is no doubt we lost business because of our geographic location, but we also won business because of it as some of our clients enjoyed escaping London to spend time with us in the Hampshire countryside, 50 miles south of London. In some cases our clients lived nearer to us than London, so working in our office on a Friday would provide them with a faster route home from work. The other advantage we had, was excellent access to talent in our region and a lower staff turnover than that of London Agencies.

But would we do it the same if we had our time again?

In terms of lifestyle, our offices were as near to our front doors as possible though in retrospect we think that we'd have grown bigger, faster if we had started in London or another major city.

We knew that for our Agency to be scalable we needed to move to London or a major/international city (or very close suburbs with less than a 30 minutes commute).

Once you scale to £2.5m it's a good idea to choose a major city for a first or second office and build a 50-50 team over the two locations. It won't be easy managing your Agency over two or more locations, but it's achievable.

You can still scale an Agency in a regional location. Most of our clients are based in regional UK areas between one and three hours from London, yet they are all performing very well and boasting higher than average staff retention and a healthier work-life integration. They still all acknowledge, however, that were they to scale their Agency even further, it would be a great help to have a London office

The concentration of larger international businesses is weighted towards London and the surrounding areas, so London has almost a separate economy to the rest of the country. Yes, when we ran our Agency, we didn't initially feel the need for a London presence, as most of our clients were happy to travel out to the country to see us. Some of your London clients will also enjoy the experience of travelling out of London to visit your other office but perhaps not every time they need to see you!

With the hindsight and experience of being involved in other successful Agencies, if we had to start again it would be in London or a major city. Don't be afraid to start there if you can, rather than regret it later because you find yourself needing to move offices, yet unable to because many of your team don't want to leave.

It is not a secret, and indeed not a coincidence, that most large Agencies have their UK headquarters in London. Agencies here attract international business, top class talent, and more significant budgets than you are likely to find elsewhere.

London's high concentration of talent, and the opportunities it offers to win more substantial new business, is no doubt advantageous as you scale, and offers your business a certain sense of security

Some clients who like very regular contact may only deal with Agencies close to them and will often want to use your offices as their own. Other clients may not care about location at all, as long as you can meet up somewhere.

There are Agencies all over the UK, and of course there is talent outside of London.

But if you feel geography is limiting the growth of your Agency then consider creating a new office and extending your reach to new customers.

The main point is you don't need to be in a city, but inevitably it will help. We also know others who have been able to win huge accounts, despite being based in obscure locations. Their talent speaks for itself. But for others, it works to start regionally and then create a capital, or significant city, base. Those that do often scale bigger and faster as a result.

If you aspire to ultimately sell your Agency one day, then being located in a capital or having a significant city presence can be the added premium to your sale price.

One Vision

We are big believers that the clearer your vision the more likely it is to happen. Having a vision will help you focus more clearly on your personal goals, indeed everything you do subconsciously will be working towards them. We often have to explain, "If you don't know where you are going, well you just won't get there!". How clear are you about your personal and business life road map?

We highly recommend that you undertake the following exercise.

It's simple and very effective.

It's important you find some quiet place away from everything and everyone to complete this task, giving yourself some "me time". It's imperative that you can visualise your future clearly and try to create the image of your life in your head to help you with getting all the details down.

The objective of this exercise is to create two short PowerPoint or Keynote presentations, or for those with a more creative approach, feel free to create a mood board.

The first presentation titled

"My personal life (and family) in three to five (and 10 if you can) years from now."

Some ideas to include (try to think of each of these in as much details as possible):

- Where do you see yourself living?

- Who is with you? Family/friends?

- What car do you drive?

- What personal interests/hobbies do you pursue?

- Where do you holiday/how do you travel?

- How much are you earning?

- Do you volunteer or support causes?

- What's important to you?

The second presentation titled

"Your Agency business in three and five (and 10 if you'd like) years from now."

Again, be as specific as you can, some ideas to include:

- How many people in your team?

- Where is the office or offices located?

- What do they look like?

- What are your revenues?

- What are you famous or infamous for?

- What are you an expert in?

- What is your role in the company?

- Where are you based?

- What will you do to ensure you are investing in yourself on this journey?

- What skills would you have learnt?

- What hurdles would you have to overcome?

- How are you viewed professionally?

- What would make you have a sense of achievement or success or recognition?

Try to review these annually, make sure you are on track and realign/evolve the plan as you move through the years, and your aspirations change or get clearer.

MEET BEAT

Time and time again we meet with Agencies and their teams who don't know their sales targets. We think this story highlights the importance of setting targets and the impact it can have:

When we were a six-man Agency, we regularly turned over about £20,000 per month, but this was pretty much a break-even figure as staff costs and overheads were about £18,000 per month.

We were continually unable to pay ourselves due to cash flow being tight. The small level of profit was struggling to turn to cash, given client's payment terms which were usually 45-60 days.

At this stage we appointed a Non-Exec. We couldn't afford him, but he brought us a piece of new business, which covered his cost immediately.

The first thing he observed was that we had forgotten to set sales targets, sounds incredible right? We just couldn't see the wood from the trees, and in our heads, we only saw the break-even number as the number we needed to reach monthly.

As we were regularly selling £20,000 per month, the first thing the Non-Exec did was to get something visual which we could all see, which happened to be a flip chart showing us hitting £22,000 that month.

Guess what? We hit £22,000. The next month he tasked us to hit £24,000. We reached £24,000 in sales.

This process repeated itself, and from the June when he first came in to help the following January, the business went from £20,000 a month to £42,000. We doubled the business in just over six months, just from being given a number to focus on.

Having made sure that appropriate business targets were set, all that was left was to adjust the business mindset. We truly feel that you can achieve what you believe you can. If you are stuck on a low turnover, just thinking of a more significant figure that you'd like to turnover is half the battle.

We suddenly became profitable, and the cash started to follow the profits.

60 months of targets later we hit a run rate of £3.5m.

Once you've set a target, make sure everyone in the business knows what it is, every month, from now on.

So, what do you do when you miss targets?

The important thing to note about targets is that it is much easier to build from where you currently are, than where you need to be. We've been into many Agencies where, let's say, their current sales number is circa £100,000 a month, but instead of their next target being £110,000 it's £150,000, a number they keep missing.

However they need to hit that higher sales number because the team and overheads were built around it. As we said earlier - always recruit behind the sales curve, remembering that it's better to find new business and then recruit a team in line with the increased sales, rather than recruit a bigger team and wait for the sales to land, as this could be costly financially. And if your sales are lower than your overheads then you need to have a plan to either cut costs or fund a slower recovery on the sales number.

So always set your targets in line with your current sales performance and build from there.

The other problem with chasing unrealistic sales targets is that, as you constantly miss them, your business starts to lose confidence and you start to become a little needier when selling.

You may not even realise the psychological and behavioural changes that happen to you, but your prospects will.

The principle is that you first need a target you can hit, and then you beat it. Then raise it as the example above showed. If you are missing sales targets, you may need to lower your target to the last three months average number, cut your costs to that figure and rebuild from a position of strength.

FOCUS, FOCUS, FOCUS

If there was one piece of advice that we've taken from successful entrepreneurs, the ones who have achieved a high level of success, it's "Focus!".

For many entrepreneurs and business owners, the buzz of seeing a new venture in everything you do can be a focus killer. For Agencies, this is even more of a challenge. We often have clients offering us joint ventures. The ideas themselves plus the excitement of doing something new, mixed in with the opportunity to own a product business is so compelling.

When presented with these opportunities, particularly in today's world of the fast-paced transformation of brands, products and service; it's especially hard to resist the temptation of wanting to get involved. Then there's the nagging sense that a product business would be a much simpler business.

We now want to share some examples with you of Agencies we have been so close to that we know the full facts. We also know of many others with similar stories.

Agency A:

A member of the team has an idea; the Agency founder backs them as long as they work on the concept in their spare time. The original Agency grows to £2m and the other business grows to almost £6m, the team member leaves and the business is run separately by the team member. The new business then sells for £12m, £6m each. The Agency owner still focuses on the Agency, and it grows to a value of £4m.

The sensible lesson to take from this is that the Agency owner empowered the team member to run the other business as a separate entity, so the Agency owner did not lose focus and achieve a successful outcome.

Agency B:

The owner invested in a product business when the 10-year old Agency was circa £1.2m. The other product business starts to take up a lot of their time and focus. The Agency almost went out of business, which was a wake-up call for them. The Agency owner now focuses on the Agency solely and as a result, that Agency grew to £4m in just three years.

The key lesson here, often missed when a business fails, is that the owner does not truly understand why it failed. This means the owner/shareholders aren't able to learn from the mistake and are therefore likely to repeat it.

The lesson here was that the owner should have focused on one business at a time; the outstanding results for the business post administration speak for themselves.

Agency C:

The Agency owner had developed a content management product. The Agency owner's message, when talking about the business publicly, was confusing as people were unsure whether they had an Agency or a content management system (CMS) business. He finally stopped focusing on the CMS business and now the Agency has grown from six staff to 30 staff.

The lesson here is that when you are selling your service, your prospects want you to be clear and concise about what you are selling; similarly, the people in the team need to be sure about which business they work for.

Agency D:

The Agency creates a software application and spends 10 years with a team size of 12, unable to break through and grow. The co-founder, and shareholder, leave the business and take the software application with them.

The software application grows to a £40m business. The remaining business partner then focuses back on the Agency and, with this renewed focus, grows sales to £4.5m with a team of 50.

By changing the two businesses operating as one, to two businesses operating independently, both companies were able to get the focus they deserved and immediately started to flourish and grow in both size and value.

It's true that some Intellectual Property (IP) in a core product or service at the heart of your offering can help your business valuation, but more than often it's an unnecessary distraction to your business focus, and one which may complicate a potential exit. We would always advise you speak to a Mergers and Acquisitions (M&A) specialist before putting IP at the heart of your Agency growth plans to check it's not in-fact going to harm the value of the business long term.

Try to make sure that the IP is part of your core proposition, not a separate entity; unless you are specifically advised to do so for tax purposes.

The age of Agencies at the heart of digital transformation is now upon us, and as such there are more distractions than ever, as well as conversations about Agencies moving to products' businesses. Our only words are that the grass may turn out to be greener for some, but for others it may very well prove to be an even more significant challenge to running an Agency - despite how good making the change might seem initially on paper.

Chapter 3: Money, Money, Money

FIFTEEN MINUTE FINANCE

The structure of your finance team depends on many variables such as business size, client numbers and the type of accounting package used.

Our book, which mostly advises companies generating (or planning to generate) revenues between £50,000 and £5m, will show you how many people you will need to work on your company finances at any one time, matching the level of resources to the size of business.

We feel your finance team should be able to provide an MD with any vital financial information within 15 minutes. If they can't, then either the employees are prioritising incorrectly, or you require more staff, or a different kind of employee.

Stage 1:

For a business generating revenue of up to £250,000, we typically find that either Agency owners or family members do the books. Or worse, that finances get left to the accountant at the end of the year, which is definitely not something that we would recommend!

If this applies to you, we recommend you hire a bookkeeper, even if just for two-four hours per week. This will ensure that you are on top of the success of your company, a professional job is being done and your time is freed up for other areas of the business.

Finance needn't be done at snail's pace through a manual input of information into Excel. We tell clients to install programmes such as Xero accounting software. It is easy to use for invoicing and imports your bank transactions straight into the accounting system. By cutting down the time it takes to do accounts substantially, you can employ a bookkeeper for half the time, and they will still have time to do other useful tasks for your company.

It may sound unnecessary, but we would urge you to think about employing a separate credit controller for chasing up any outstanding payments. It can get awkward asking people you are working with for money. The solution is simple: have someone else do it. This sensitive job is best left to the pros.

At this level, it is unlikely you will be able to afford a Financial Director, and that is fine. If it is the choice between an FD and a Credit Controller, go for the Credit Controller every time.

Stage 2:

For businesses generating revenue of around £750,000 to £1m a year and upwards, you should employ a full-time Finance Manager for at least 30 hours per week. This person should be handling all of your finances, including some administration tasks such as insurances, and office and facilities management.

At this stage you should also seriously consider having a Financial Director (even if just for one day a month) to analyse the business and ensure everything is running smoothly, a bit like a foreman in a factory.

It is still useful to have a separate Credit Controller, but if the Finance Manager has experience in debt collection, that can be beneficial too.

Good Finance Managers are as hard to find as needles in a haystack. If they are talented other companies won't want to let them go.

The right finance person also has to fit your company's culture. Some have their way of working which may not work with your company, and the right culture fit is of great importance to your company and its employees.

You will advertise this role when your company is going through a lot of change, which unfortunately is a disadvantage.

Understandably, the right people may not want to work with a company in flux, as this creates an extra heavy workload due to an increasing payroll, cash flow issues, new clients, and all manner of other changes. Don't give up though. The person you hire here could be the very change your company needs.

Stage 3:

If your turnover is £1.5 million or above, then your finance team should include at least a Finance Manager, a part time Credit Controller and a Financial Director who spends at least a couple of days a month on the business.

It may be advisable to get a Finance Assistant. This is dependent on the workload, as having multiple clients and staff will require multiple people to keep on top of invoices, payroll, and supplier payments.

We will approach debt collection in a separate section of this book, but at this level it is appropriate to formalise the way you collect debts from clients.

Attributes of a finance person

It is crucial when employing people in your finance department that, not only do they have the right sort of personality, but that your Finance Managers and directors provide you with the best information to do your business well. Unfortunately, this is not always the case.

There are two types of finance people:

1. Traditionalists:

These guys only do finance reports and numbers. Technically they are fulfilling their job description, but it's a limited approach and not ideal.

2. Commercially aware:

These people go above and beyond to help you understand the importance of finance on your business. They help you understand why things happen, what the reports show and where to improve.

You will benefit from recruiting people who will help you understand and interpret the intricacies of finance. These recruits will be exposed to how businesses really work and their contribution will be much more constructive than just creating lots of reports.

Picking the best people for the job

When recruiting a full-time finance person, you have to make sure that they are right for your company. This doesn't mean years of experience, or the highest qualifications possible. You are not necessarily looking for a fully qualified Chartered Accountant; you are looking for someone who can both do the job and also happily go to the pub with you and your team.

The most successful finance people integrate themselves into the business and form good working relationships with other areas of the business such as delivery, sales and marketing.

Whoever you employ will be talking to clients and handling invoices. They talk to your suppliers. They will see how much everyone gets paid, including you. They will have access to the company accounts. They therefore, have to be entirely trustworthy and you will need a good relationship with them. It isn't only about keeping your finance manager sweet; it helps if you genuinely like them.

When we first recruited someone in this role for Bluhalo, we made some errors. The initial mistake was hiring someone who was not a good culture fit. It therefore shouldn't have come as a surprise when the person in question popped out for a baked potato and literally, never came back. They were so out of their comfort zone it would be unfair to blame them.

Ultimately, finance should be about smart cash-flow management, accurate books and reporting, and helping you to grow the business. All the rest is about personality. It is best to surround yourself with people you want to work with.

MEET THE BANKER

It is a common misconception for Agencies that you don't need banking facilities to run efficiently. In fact, it is highly likely you will need a business overdraft, loan, or another form of borrowing at some point during your Agency life-cycle. This is particularly true when you face times of decline, rapid growth or a client taking longer to pay you than anticipated. There are various situations when you may require a cash injection or working capital support.

If you do not have the comfort of these banking facilities on hand then you are at risk of not paying your staff, forced to make redundancies, paying tax late and incurring fines; or paying suppliers late and destroying relationships. Poor cash management can create or accelerate the decline. Given the choice wouldn't you prefer to just get some security in place?

So, what to choose?

The overdraft:

It is good to have support from the bank; but how much? We advise that you have in place banking facilities to the value of between one month's payroll costs and one month's turnover. In our opinion, having an overdraft facility agreed with the bank (which is for short-term cash pain) is a wise move. Most banks will offer an overdraft facility of up to £25,000 without you having to secure it, by putting a charge over your personal assets. You will normally just have to sign a personal guarantee, which is a promise to repay the bank personally should the business fail. It is sometimes better than taking a loan, as you will otherwise be paying a percentage of interest on money that you may not immediately need.

The bank loan:

In our opinion a bank loan is best used in the following situations:

Long-term investment purchase; for example, buying another business; debt consolidation; where you have some smaller loans; or a large overdraft that you can't get rid of and need another route; or financing an office move, which can require a significant upfront capital outlay

To secure a loan, the lender would often require some form of security. If your business assets are higher than the amount you need to borrow it is likely your loan application will be accepted, but with the bank taking a debenture, which is a legal charge, over the assets of the company.

If, however you had, for example, £25k of business assets and needed a loan of £100k, then you might face some difficulty. To obtain credit approval, the bank would ask the company directors to offer their personal assets as security against the business loan.

The bank overdraft and traditional bank loan are usually offered by the mainstream business banks. We go on to talk more about alternative forms of finance below, but before we do that, we often get asked - who are the best banks? We don't usually recommend one bank over another; it's more about finding the best bank managers to work with, from a mindset, personality and experience perspective. Asking three or four contacts, through word of mouth will help you find a good bank manager. If you get on with your manager, there is a higher chance of a good working relationship with the bank as a whole.

Other forms of finance:

Invoice discounting:

Invoice discounting is a financial transaction where a business 'sells' its debtor book (i.e., invoices outstanding from clients) to a funder. The funder provides financing to the seller of the accounts, in the form of a cash 'advance'. For example, if you have a debtor book of £100k, some funders will buy this debt from you and advance at a level of 50%, giving you £50k. Once the clients have paid, the funder is repaid in full, plus interest and charges.

This can be done by borrowing against the full debtor book, or by funding single or multiple invoices.

All banks offer invoice discounting, but due to the nature of Agency work, many are not able to fund it. Thankfully, there are some banks, willing to offer this service to Agencies.

Some of them have online platforms which integrate straight into your accounting system, making this somewhat painless.

It may not be the cheapest form of borrowing, but it has benefits such as low personal guarantees, and these facilities grow with the business. As the debtor books increases (because you will be billing more if you are scaling) you can borrow more, the amount you can borrow being based on a percentage of the entire debtor book value.

Alternative financial institutions:

There are other alternative lenders out there, who do not have a high street presence, and who tend to be more flexible than the high street banks. We should point, out of course, that this flexibility does come at a price, as on the whole they are more expensive than their high street counterparts.

But, they can make decisions more quickly, will look more favourably on businesses in challenging situations and sometimes take less security. At the time of writing this book, some of these lenders in the UK, to name just a few, were:

- Funding Circle

- Lending Crowd

- EZbob

- IWOCA

- Capital on Tap

NOT SO BOARD MEETINGS

A board meeting is a formal meeting of a company's board of Directors and shareholders, gathering to discuss the performance of their business. If any decisions are made during the meeting, then the directors have to see that they are carried out, even the Directors who found themselves too hungover or tied-up to have attended the meeting!

All companies, although not legally required to, should have at least one board meeting every year. In our opinion, however, it is much more efficient for your company to hold a board meeting every month.

Business owners are often at a disadvantage, when it comes to knowing how to improve their business, because they do not often have an opportunity to stand back and objectively review what is going on inside the company. Board meetings give business owners this perspective opportunity, and also allow directors with a fresh pair of eyes to analyse how the company is really doing; providing you with objective knowledge.

Board meetings are your one opportunity a month to get to stand back and work 'on' your business rather than from 'within it'. A typical agenda would look as follows:

Agenda

- Apologies for absence.

- Approval of previous meeting's minutes and matters arising from last meeting.

- Urgent business.

- Finance - review of company finances.

- Legal - discussion point for any lawsuits, employment contracts for directors, moving offices etc.

- Sales - review of pipeline.

- Marketing - review of marketing activity.

- HR / People - recruitment of new employees, staff morale, potential disciplinary matters.

- Operations - review of delivery and IT related items.

- Any other business.

- Close of business.

HAVING A PLAN

Budgeting

As board advisors, one of the first questions we ask on appointment is: how much do you want to grow by and how quickly?

People tend to have general targets, for example reaching a £2m turnover or a desire to sell for £10m. These kind of goals obviously won't happen overnight; in reality they are likely to take three to four years to achieve, sometimes longer. However, putting annual budgets and forecasts in place means that these goals can become a reality sooner.

Developing realistic budgets can only be done by existing companies, who can base their targets on past experiences. New companies will have to accept an element of increased guesswork.

Forecasts

If your growing business is comparable to a journey then a forecast will be your map, or a sat-nav, or a nagging partner acting as a backseat driver. There are two types of projections which your Agency should be looking at in order to grow.

The profit and loss account forecast:

This is simply a model of how the profit and loss of the company will look over a period of one year, usually aligned with the accounting year.

You begin with how you think the sales figures for the year will pan out. Start at a level roughly similar to where you are now, and if you are growing business, gradually increase those numbers through the year at a realistic pace.

You would then add in all of your current costs and allow for growth. As an example, if a service business such as an Agency increases turnover then staff numbers will need to increase, which will then drive up costs. If staff numbers increase then you may need to move office; think about this in your plan.

A sense check of this forecast is to view your overall overhead costs and aim for a 15% net profit margin (which is a healthy set of numbers for a growing Agency). And also check to see if the resulting sales targets needed to achieve this level of profits is realistic. Is your target for new business unrealistic?

For example, if your turnover has increased steadily at 20% per annum for the last three or four years, it would be considered unrealistic to put a forecast in place for the coming year that sees the business double in size.

You also need to monitor your actual financial performance each month against your budget, to see if you are on track or off track with your plan. The financial software Xero is particularly useful in reporting on this.

Make sure you keep up-to-date figures. You always need to know if you are in profit or not and figures which were up to date three months ago are not useful now. We recommend having your accounts completed within two weeks of month end to ensure that the information you are working with is as up-to-date as possible.

As a service business, you need to keep control of your costs to ensure you make a profit. If you have spent too much, you have to then ask why. There may be rational explanations for your added costs, but sometimes, the overspend is not easily identified, and you will then have to work out why there are variances between your targets, what actually happened and the consequences for the remainder of the year.

For this, you should think in thousands of pounds, not petty cash. If you are within £2-£3,000 of your overall target, then you have little to worry about. Try not to get too concerned if the amount you spend on tea bags increases, unless it becomes more than 5% of your turnover!

Cashflow forecast:

Incredibly important yet used by few businesses, a cash-flow forecast looks at the amount of money your company is in possession of at any one time and how that maps out in the short to medium term. The profit and loss forecast won't do this, as there is a distinct difference between profit and loss and cash surpluses and deficits.

It is easy for a company to make £100,000 in sales and feel as though they are financially secure, but often you won't have this money in the bank till the end of the project in a few months time (provided all goes to plan, and the work is completed). Successful businesses put themselves at risk when they have not managed to balance their income and outgoings correctly.

One of the most significant problems Agencies report when we first meet them, is cash-flow. Ninety percent of the time this problem could be resolved by getting a Credit Controller in, or by arranging sufficient working capital.

The cash-flow forecast is your early warning system. It lets you know when your clients will pay you, when you can pay suppliers, tax and staff costs.

We recommend analysing your cash-flow on at least a rolling three-month basis; this is particularly crucial for new and growing businesses. If week eight of 12 looks problematic, then you will know this in advance and can prepare in the month leading up to it so you are able to pay wages etc.

One of our clients was weak financially, and one day the accounts department announced that they were £30,000 short of paying wages. While this demonstrates why you should read the following section about hiring the right people for the job, ie those won't land you in it, it also shows why you need to plan ahead. The owners of the business mentioned above were forced to immediately inject all the money from their savings into the company. Stressful, ridiculous and entirely preventable, it was just luck that they happened to have enough to survive.

A cash-flow forecast should be in your daily routine as an owner but do it properly or again there is little value in it. Take a quick look back at last month by all means, but then keep looking forward. Keep tracking and planning so that whatever happens has been planned for, to the best of your ability.

MONTHLY REPORTING

The importance of monthly reporting is linked both to the importance of budgeting and forecasting, and to the importance of board meetings.

If you don't know the current position of your business and where you intend to go, how can you possibly get there? It would be about as pointless as spending a day on the road driving around with no intended destination. You need a target, a goal.

This section indicates useful ways of analysing your business, which any good Financial Director can and should do. Just looking at bank statements will not help you get a good indication of how on-target your business is regarding profit. All businesses need to measure their profits using monthly reporting, and larger companies should include a quarterly review which contains much greater detail and analysis of the business.

Quarterly reports are the best indication of your company's success and failures. Your business will appear in monthly reports to do better at different times of the year. January may seem a good month because a lot of projects are won. However, March may look particularly profitable, as this is the month the January projects are completed and you get paid. August may seem bad as most of your staff and clients will be away on holiday, and December tends to look poorer due to its being a three-week working month. From month to month there may be peaks and troughs, but quarterly reviews manage to iron out any peaks and troughs in trading.

Agency success is very much based on staff performance and motivation. You profit by how much you sell a project for, minus the time it takes for your team to produce the work. So the most significant outgoing cost for an Agency is the payroll and it is therefore vital to achieve the perfect staff over income balance.

Get out your calculator and try this Cactus formula:

Last three months Staff Costs (including NI and Director's drawings) ÷ Last three months Gross Profits = ??%

You should have produced a percentage. If the figure is between 60-65% well done, your business income to staff ratio is where it needs to be.

If you have achieved lower than 60%, then we suggest you offer sincere apologies to your poor, overworked, or potentially underpaid staff! Achieving less than the target percentage means that you have a high work to staff ratio. This stress puts you at risk of losing your valuable employees, as well as your clients, due to poor quality or late work produced. This is particularly important if you are going to sell your Agency.

Buyers may value your company far higher if you have a low staff turnover percentage and a core team of people have been with you for years. Moreover, constant recruiting is expensive with recruitment fees as high as 20% of a salary. Even then a new employee may take two to three months to learn the ropes and get fully up to speed from a productivity perspective.

There is a little bit of leeway for those of you who have achieved a percentage of between 65-70%. For example, staff costs in London are higher, or you may have taken on a new highly paid employee who will eventually become fully productive and contribute to income.

However if your sums produced around 75% or more then you are not making enough money to cover the wages you are paying out.

Either you are inefficient in delivering work, and it takes ten of your staff to do what five can do, or you are not selling enough, or you are undercharging.

Also consider how much you are charging your clients, either as a day rate and or as a project fee. Valuing your work correctly is vital for companies. You don't want to be over the top, but you do need to achieve what you and your work are worth.

MILESTONES

Payment stages

When you negotiate any deal, it is always good practice to organise payment stages, and have a written contract, or you will find yourself on the back foot. You need to increase your business security by ensuring you have good cash-flow.

An Agency gets paid from three main sources; its project work, retainers and on the management fees on paid media spend. We will now look at the ways you can arrange your payment stages practically, so that everyone is happy.

Project work is where you have an agreed income, based on a certain amount of work over a period of time.

We would recommend that you agree on payment milestones for a project, that are in line with deliverables, always weighted in your favour so that you are paid in advance of doing any work. If you work in sprints perhaps consider matching billing in this way.

Payment milestones include:

- Some money upfront, especially for new clients (typically 20-25%).

- A sum when the design is agreed - clients may pull out here due to the subjectivity of designs.

- More when the project is built and tested.

- More when it goes live (you should have been paid 95% at least by this point).

- Take the final small payment when the project is finished and has been running successfully for a couple of weeks.

Retainers are where a customer has booked out a certain amount of your time, paying a certain amount in advance each month (possibly every quarter if it is a small sum), until the length of the contract is finished. Again, if the contract is cancelled you can still bill for the work that was agreed.

You may be tempted to discount your work per hour for your retainer clients, as in return you receive a guaranteed income. Do not do yourself an injustice, however. The best retainer you can have is where you get as much money as possible, while keeping your client happy. This is done through negotiations, where both parties feel like they are benefitting, or else the relationship could turn sour.

Media and partner spend is money paid through you on behalf of the client to market sites on media channels. This includes items such as television advertising, print or paid social advertising and paid search engine positioning, etc. For this, you would take money from the client upfront to reduce any risk to you. For marketing on Google, Facebook and others, clients could spend hundreds of thousands on any one project. If you were expected to put this money up yourself, and then the client pulled out or went into administration, you would be at risk of the same. Perhaps consider getting a charge card (such as American Express) to aid cash flow on this (giving you and the team the extra benefit of rewards points). Or even better, ask the client to fund the media spend themselves so that you avoid any cash flow issues.

Contracts

A contract is a written agreement between the customer and supplier, setting out the work that will be completed, how much will be charged, when payments will be made and may also include provisions for dealing with disputes between each side.

If you are in possession of signed contracts, an Agency is more comfortable in the sales it has achieved. If you aim to make £2.5m in a year, and your existing customers have signed £1.9m of contracts already, then your business is given confidence.

Without a contract, clients can say they don't want to work with you anymore and refuse to pay you what was agreed. If the same occurs when you have a contract, you can continue billing until the end of the contract and have more time to replace the client once the contract ends.

In the contract, you can state how much you will be paid for a certain amount of work. The client then will have to pay you more for any extra work requested. In other words the client cannot mess you about, your company will be more secure and everyone knows where they stand.

Negotiations these days are gentle affairs; there is no need for demands and aggression. You will usually strike a deal that works well for both parties, relatively easily. In this case, negotiation training may be a good investment for you and some of your staff. It's not a done deal until contracts are signed, sealed and delivered; so ensure your team know how to close a deal, and that nothing can jeopardise it once you've won the pitch.

The key to contracts is keeping up to date. Keep abreast of any changing legalities and make sure your contracts are in line with your business growth. What is right for you now is probably not the same as it was when you were a one-man band. This is especially true for example if the services of your Agency change, for example, offline to online.

Things change, and people do not always honour agreements. Contracts are protection. It is still worth getting a friendly lawyer onside to regularly check your contracts and the terms and conditions.

GROWING THROUGH THE NUMBERS

The finance teams should be working closely with both the new business teams and the Account Managers to help them determine new targets. Each year there should be a guaranteed amount of money from existing customer contracts, a target for Account Managers to sell even more to their existing clients, and a target for new business teams.

New business targets are based on the hope that new business comes in smoothly throughout the year. To achieve this, monthly targets should be set. You thrive on consistent business coming in. By looking at sales lines and seeing how much the team thinks they can sell, the finance team should be able to produce realistic targets. Remember not to exaggerate your targets, as this can demoralise the new business team or make them think you don't understand their line of work.

Existing client teams, Account Managers and Directors, know they will have a certain amount of guaranteed money coming in through the year via trusted customers buying their ideas. All they must do for these clients is service and look after them. Having achieved this, they will then be expected to sell even more to existing clients throughout the year.

You should have a proactive not reactive account management.

A reactive Account Manager will assume a customer will spend money without feeling the need to ask them. It will then be a shock if the client decides to stop spending. Proactive Account Managers will be on the phone with their clients regularly and know how their client feels.

Moreover, if a client is wavering on spending money with you, the Account Manager will meet with them and give them new ideas for how to maximise their investment. If the client still doesn't want to spend, then a good Account Manager will make you aware of this, and you will have lots of time to adjust your budget and look for more clients.

To help the existing client teams, finance people should map out the predicted income, depicting the sales patterns throughout the year. This gives an idea as to where further sales can come from.

Ordinarily, good regular clients will have a budget for how much they will spend with you. When we worked with a premiership football club, we knew that every year they would spend £20,000 on a redesign, have a new kit launch at £20,000, and update their site every month for £5,000. This guaranteed Bluhalo over £100,000 a year of guaranteed income. Then we focused on the other areas they could spend with us, which actively helped them to grow.

One year our Contract Manager at the same club was leaving, and it was vital that we prepared for our account to be cancelled should the replacement Manager wish to move the account to their own preferred digital Agency. We downgraded the sum of this account in our forecast accordingly, though luckily this never happened.

Again if a big account decides to leave you, your forecast will have to be downgraded. Sometimes an Account Manager will get a gut feeling that their client is going to leave, either through the way they speak on the phone, or if they take an abnormally long time to respond to emails.

If you are prudent with your forecasts, you will always meet your targets. However be wary of being over prudent, as this would put much more pressure on the new business team to make up the difference in projected targets when it isn't necessary.

RATE SETTING

Setting your daily rate can seem difficult as there is a delicate balance between underselling yourself and overcharging. However, there is no sophisticated algorithm involved. Ultimately, when you are growing, you need to look at what other Agencies charge and ask for roughly the same amount, which is currently approximately £900-£1,000 a day.

Most Agencies have the same business structure as one another and typically make 5-20% margin on these day rates, depending on how much their staff are paid, where they are based (for example London offices and salaries are more expensive than the rest of the UK), and how good they are at delivering and managing project budgets.

As the business grows and you become more successful, you will find that you need to increase your rates in order to be able to afford to employ more talented and experienced staff.

The easiest way to increase your day rates is to have a full pipeline, allowing to gradually test the price increases on new customers.

Basing your rates on industry averages can be difficult when you are growing as an Agency, as increasing the number of people you employ can lessen your less profits. In this case, charge as much as you can, and make sure that the client is still happy to pay this amount. At times of growth, a bit of negotiation will help.

The trick here is to keep evolving your business so that you are not caught in a market which is delivering services that have become commoditised. Better to be in a market of the few, rather than a market of the many. That way, your costs cannot easily be compared to competitors, as there are fewer of them.

EBIT-DUH?

Lastly, to conclude on Agency finances, it is essential to understand how your company is valued. This gives you a scorecard to monitor how well your asset is growing in value and brings some sanity to the chaos of everyday Agency life.

The value of your company is usually based on a multiple of EBITDA i.e. your Earnings Before Interest, Tax, Depreciation and Amortisation.

Having said that most deals are usually based on a multiple of EBITDA, we do occasionally see Agencies valued on a multiple of annual revenue, which tends to be those Agencies where long contracted retained clients make up the bulk of the revenue.

EBITDA is another word for profit, used by accountants and financiers to value businesses. If you are at the sharp end of your Agency growth journey, you may have already heard of this description.

An EBITDA multiple is used as an indicator of how much a business is worth. At the moment, we see a lot of Agencies valued at between five to seven times their annual EBITDA.

In our opinion, having advised on many transactions during the last 10 years these are the key factors which affect multiples of EBITDA valuations in Agencies.

Factors which affect multiples are:

- Brand & strong Agency proposition.

- Focusing on a niche service or sector.

- Working in a space that represents cutting-edge technology.

- The strength of the management team.

- Having some awards to shout about.

- Location - being regionally based is not an issue, but having a small London presence may help.

- High day rate/high profitability.

- Having a founder who has a high profile.

Chapter 4: Sales & Marketing 101

SALES IS A DIRTY WORD

Agencies can't grow without sales, although 'sales' is often considered a dirty word by creative and technical purists, who prefer to focus on 'the work, the work, the work' and just hope that by building reputation the sales will just come.

Of course, this is a strategy of sorts, but it often means slower growth over a longer period as the Agency builds its reputation and fame.

In reality, everyone in the Agency must have a contributory role in increasing sales. We should all play a part in evangelising about what we know and create, demonstrating our capabilities to solve customer's challenges.

We all must help the Agency to build connections and trusted relationships.

We often ask Agencies to map out their sales process, to help the wider team understand their roles in sales. Sure, creative and technical types don't have to pick up the phone and cold call or email prospects, but they can create strong thought-leadership content, speak at events or help Account Managers or sales teams with an ongoing stream of ideas that could be taken to clients.

A simple yet effective example of everyone in the Agency helping on sales is ensuring that everyone on the team helps curate, repost and share content because a re-share may well strike a chord with a friend's company, or create a referred opportunity from one friend to another.

It still surprises us every single day to see Agencies' social media posts that have only two or three likes and shares, when they have a team of 30 people who could help that post potentially reach thousands of people.

There is no question that the Agencies, who have some form of sales culture underpinning their business, grow the fastest. However there is a balance to strike as you grow your Agency.

The slowest growing Agencies tend to only focus on their client base which, on the one hand means that they tend to have the highest quality work, on the other it means they may not grow their Agency as fast or attract new clients as quickly compared with others.

The best Agencies are the ones who get the right balance between new and existing client business, rather than focusing on one at the expense of the other.

Now we have explained the importance of an underlying sales culture, for those who want to scale quicker, let's now look at the sales role as you scale in the early years.

The irony with Agencies is that you may find you need fewer new business staff as you grow. This is because in the early days of an Agency, new business opportunities are higher in volume and lower in value.

For example, Agencies with revenues of £500,000, may win two to four new clients a month, whereas Agencies at £5m+ could win as few as two to four new clients per year.

There is no one fix-all solution to an Agency sales team structure, but these are the four roles we most commonly see.

The hunter

A hunter builds business connections in the places he or she wants opportunities to come from.

The hunter is often the Agency owner (or one of the founder/owners), the hunter could also be an Agency leader, industry expert, strategist or evangelist.

The hunter, socialises, speaks, evangelises in the places he or she wants opportunities to come from. They are often better at discovering, identifying or creating opportunities, rather than seeing them through to fruition.

They are usually people who are more success driven than money motivated.

They build trust and chemistry quickly and are good at building lots of contacts, they are excellent connectors of people and their contacts can often become friends and acquaintances.

The sales professional

Commonly known as the Business Development Director, Sales and Marketing Manager, Commercial Director or Head of Partnerships.

These people understand the competitive advantage of having a proper sales process, the stages of which are typically:

1. Qualifying the opportunity.
2. Communicating the Agencies proposition and solution.
3. Creating compelling deadlines to get the work started.
4. Overcoming prospects objections.
5. Negotiating.
6. Closing the opportunity.

The more personable they are and the more money motivated sales professionals are, the more successful they usually become. Commercially savvy, they can sometimes act as an intermediary between client and Agency.

The best ones can network, won't expect leads to be provided and will work prospects and clients for more referrals. Unfortunately they are not that common in our experience, the reality is that most sales professionals have an expectation that there will be some kind of marketing support in generating the leads they are to manage through their sales process.

Recruiting the right sales professional isn't easy.

Recruiting, retaining and making this role successful has been the source of much learning over the past ten or so years. So many Agencies struggle to get the right person for this role.

This is an investment hire that often takes many years to succeed.

For us, it's arguably the hardest hire, and here's why.

Firstly, most founding directors only sell £0-£100,000 in their first Agency year. Some owners achieve more than this amount, but most don't, and they forget it takes a longer time to build a B2B pipeline of services compared with a B2B one of products.

Secondly, most people in a new business role want relatively hefty salaries with additional commission paid on top.

At the end of their first year, their sales are usually below expectations and it's hard for the owner to justify the salary. And the salesperson is unhappy that he is not earning the on-target salary he wanted.

The Agency owner then puts pressure on the salesperson to increase sales, and the salesperson starts looking for a new job; in 90% of cases the new business person leaves after 14 months which is a complete waste of time and investment.

To add injury to insult, about three to four months later some of the deals that the salesperson had been developing will drop in, and you'll have regretted making the decision to let them go. If only the Agency owner had a little more patience or had set the expectation, from the outset, that within 24 months they would be bringing in at least 5x salary and by 48 months 10x salary.

Another typical situation that occurs is the salesperson arrives talking the talk, with lots of promises of guaranteed business through his or her network, but in reality is lazy, failing to deliver while continually talking about opportunities.

We are often most wary of previously very successful salespeople, who over-set the expectation of their abilities, forgetting how hard they had to work in previous roles to achieve that success.

Most sales professionals are better at managing the sales process around a lead, than they are at generating a lead themselves. Sure they will try and nurture some leads referred to them by the sales they have already created, but as the B2B cycle is fairly long, and new business people are typically not hunters, they will usually expect leads from the marketing team. Of course, there are always exceptions and the best salespeople will work harder and do some prospecting.

To make a new business hire successful, you need to find someone who is committed to at least a five-year journey, someone who wants to be locked in to and believes in, your Agency vision.

Someone, who while working for you won't feel overly pressurised (unless they ask for it), because they are incentivised to work hard!

The successful candidate is incredibly friendly, driven, hardworking and understands that while they need some quick win sales, their new business sales performance will probably look like this in relation to new business.

Year 1. £50-75k
Year 2. £100-£150k
Year 3. £200-£250k
Year 4. £500k
Year 5. £750k
Year 6. £1m

And to anyone who is now shouting "But my Business Manager did more than this in his year one!" we congratulate you both but be assured that you are the minority

The farmer

This is better known as the Client Services, Account Director or Account Manager role.

Account Managers tend not to be naturally sales focused and should be all the more treasured if they are. And in which case they can often move to new business roles better than a cold recruit). Account Managers are focused on nurturing clients. Their role is to help grow and develop relationships through the pitch stage, and they aren't usually business creators or natural closers.

Too many get wrapped up in reactively managing (or hiding behind) client work (project management), rather than being the useful proactive resource that clients, when surveyed, say they want.

Their strengths usually lie in their ability to be great communicators, build great relationships and sometimes friendships, with the Agency's clients and must focus on offering the best client experience possible.

The Agency Marketing Manager

In an Agency The Marketing Manager is probably the most important role you will ever fill. It's amazing how many Agencies don't include this role in their staffing when it is such an essential and obvious hire.

The Marketing Manager's role is simple yet key: to create a strategy, schedule a plan and then execute that strategy and plan to help the Agency find leads.

As we say in this book over and over again everything in an Agency starts with a sale, well even more importantly a sale starts with a lead. Leads create sales, sales lead to building a team and the team create the processes and deliver the services, then the cash arrives to pay for everything. Then repeat.

The Marketing Manager typically works day to day with the Founder, or members of staff who are most aligned to the hunter role and farmer roles. That said, the Marketing Manager who gets the whole team to support him or her will often achieve the greatest success. These are the Agencies who will often have the best sales cultures where everyone is supporting lead generation in some way. The golden rule regarding The Marketing Manager role is as soon as you can afford, or cash allows you to recruit for this role, do it!

The pitch team

A group of people from the Agency, who can collectively quickly build chemistry/trust, and prove to any prospective client that they are the right team, and have the right capabilities, to deliver the results the client needs.

The pitch team can consist of Agency Owners/ Directors/ Hunters, Sales Professionals and Account Managers, Project Managers, Strategist, Creatives, Techies and more. The larger the Agency, the less likely the owners are to be involved, but clients may require their presence during meetings to validate that they are an important account. The key is to get the right people in the room and match roles and personalities at all levels.

ONE BILLION POUNDS

We've worked with over 1,000+ Agencies over the past 10 years, and we always ask them how and where their new business comes from. Every few months we discover a new technique and add it to our methodology!

We've taken the data from a cumulative total of over £1 billions' worth of pipeline opportunities, in order to work out what the most common lead sources are for Agency new business wins.

Frequently when we have our first contact with any Agency and ask where their leads come from, the Agency owner says, "We get all our business from word of mouth referrals", and then they apologise for it. We remind them that there is absolutely nothing wrong with this as the majority of the largest Agency clients' relationships started with trusted referrals or connections.

Through this extensive research, we have identified four key areas of lead generation.

Not everyone will be aligned precisely with these four areas for lead generation. Most Agencies we begin working with are only getting revenue from two of the four areas. Embrace these four areas for lead generation and you will solve most of your Agency new business challenges, which in turn will help you fix the rest of your Agency's challenges.

Finally, it's also worth remembering that as Agencies and professional service businesses, we are mostly selling services in Agencies rather than products and that services are sold differently to products. This means that leads need to be generated using very different techniques for Agencies than those used for product businesses.

Professional services are sold:

1. Through having trust and chemistry with a prospective client (chemistry).

2. By demonstrating the capability to solve the client's requirements (credentials or creds).

Selling a service by establishing both chemistry and credentials is essential. If you have both, then you are in the best position to generate a lead and a sale.

As it's essential for those working in Agency new business to build trust and chemistry with their clients and prospects, we wanted to share with you some of the different approaches of how trust can be created.

The following image shows the pillars of trust.

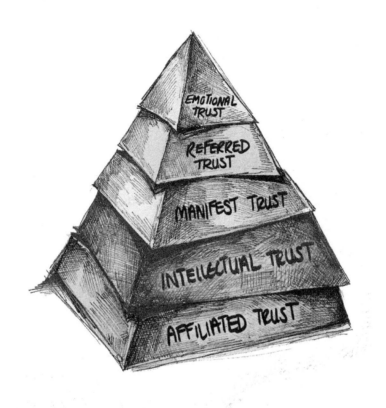

Trusted referral

Most Agencies we meet for the first time will describe their primary new business lead source as "coming from referrals".

To create referrals, you must have connections with people who have trust in you, your reputation and your abilities.

Emotional trust

You create this trust through an emotional connection, perhaps through a friend, an ex (or current) work colleague or maybe a client who you have a strong relationship with. It could also be someone who you have shared some kind of personal experience with, someone that you have something in common with, which creates that personal connection.

Experiences can include celebrating anniversaries, winning awards together or helping your clients look good in their jobs by perhaps letting their boss know how great they have been to work with on a project.

Manifest trust

This form of trust is built from being an expert in your field. You may deliver this expertise through written thought-leadership or by being a public speaker, which will create the impression that you are an authority in the area that you work in and in turn you build trust through your expertise.

There has been a shift more recently by Agency owners, building strong personal brand identities such as Stephen Bartlett at Social Chain and Gary Vaynerchuk of Vayner Media. This is something we would urge all Agency owners to consider creating, albeit in a very personal way. It doesn't necessarily have to be highly extroverted or an outspoken approach.

Many people are writing titles like "if you don't have a strong personal brand by 2020 you won't be trusted to work with". We'll see about that one, nevertheless developing your personal brand is one action to be embraced.

Affiliated trust

Affiliated trust is formed when you offer a specific service, or you meet someone who has a particular need, and they realise you can solve their problem.

They may have been searching for someone to solve this specific problem, and through this serendipitous chance encounter with you (their problem solver!), there is an immediate sense of trust that is created.

Intellectual trust

Intellectual trust is formed between two experts. Dr Robert Cialdini in his book 'Influence' references the importance of displaying credentials clearly to build trust.

The best example of this is usually "I'm a Doctor, and you are a Doctor" we both studied in the same way; therefore there is mutual respect and trust built through a shared journey of education and profession.

In an Agency, intellectual trust is gained by building solid credentials, and having owners building their profiles with non-exec or consulting roles to other companies. In addition they may hold trade body positions and certifications from partners or suppliers that validate their expertise. Of course, with CEO to CEO there is a professional connection too as empathy is created between both people.

Trust is also built by helping others, although we often refer to this as reciprocity, the science of helping others creates a social behaviour for others to reciprocate.

Trust at all times must be authentic and we recommend you invest time in learning how to build trust quickly as it's a very powerful ally in Agency life where often you have to build trust with a prospect over the course of a few short meetings.

Finally, Spencer would like to share an example of how building chemistry and trust helped him win one of his first large deals.

"I was pitching for a premiership football club website, and the original list of Agencies invited to pitch was long. I was shortlisted down from 18 to 12 then finally to the last 4. I was disappointed that it was not from 12 straight down to one and decided to pull out of the pitch. We had invested too much time and money already. The football club convinced us to stay in as they said we were 'one of their favourites going into the final round'. We had just won another deal with a motorsport company, and I saw an opportunity to take the decision maker of the football club to one of their motorsport events so he could potentially meet other corporate sponsors.

On the trip, we got to spend more time with the prospect, and we were able to get him to spend social time with us and learn more about the type of people we were. We were a strong cultural fit and good guys and he got to see that we were not just suppliers. We built a business friendship and trust which led to him asking if "I give you this opportunity will you deliver?" 100% we replied, and we went on to win the deal.

We built trust by helping him, and he got to know us and validate our expertise and the value we could add to the relationship too.

We currently work with a client in our consulting business, who says that it takes him around five meetings with the prospect for enough trust to be built to win the deal.

To reiterate an earlier point, always remember you have a much better chance of a successful outcome if you can find something in common with the people you are looking to build trust with.

Finally, credentials are built through your ability to demonstrate and promote your capabilities, often through case studies, awards entries and showreels."

Method one: The 30/30/30/10 (™) Cactus

This method outlines the four areas we identified after researching patterns where leads originated from on hundreds of Agency's pipelines.

30% of leads originated from existing client referrals or where clients change employment and ask you to pitch at their new company.

30% of leads originated from strategic partnerships: alliances with other companies; leveraging each other's brands, services and trust for mutual gain. A strategic partnership is where you work with another company for mutual gain. Partnerships only ever work where both parties are equally engaged in the partnership.

30% from NEST, which stands for **N**etworking (or Socialising), putting on your own **E**vents, Public **S**peaking all underpinned by written **T**hought leadership pieces/expertise.

10% of leads come from search engines (paid and organic), social media, phone marketing, PR, newsletters, direct mail, entering awards, building fame, and website enquiries.

Yes only 10%! However this 10% is extremely important as it helps generate continual marketing touch-points, content that reminds your clients and prospects of your services.

Something to note is that when analysed closely most leads that are reported to have come from a particular lead source have actually originated from somewhere else, so always triple check for the facts!

For example, someone who hears you speak at an event, then sends you a LinkedIn message is a NEST sourced lead rather than a lead from the 10% area.

Method two: Fame

Building fame and recognition for your Agency can take many years to grow to a point where the leads are flowing in. In fact, for most Agencies fame is probably a minimum 10-year journey.

Start by investing both your marketing budget and time to generate potential award-winning work from your Agency team. Focus on promoting everything you do, whether it is work for a client or an internal project. Aim to press release the work.

Then, through internal and external managed PR and Award Entries, increase your Agency brand awareness with your target audience. This strategy will attract fame clients (we'll cover client's types later in this book) who will want to work with you.

Setting yourself targets to win high profile awards within set timeframes, will also help you focus and measure success.

Method three: Case study, focused targeting & direct /social selling.

This lead-generation technique is used more by larger Agencies. It creates a more 'outbound marketing' approach on the whole. Rather than the other approaches that aim to drive lead generation from inbound marketing.

The approach is essentially one where you create high quality case studies and sales materials (this includes putting these on your website) and distribute the content, which are highly relevant to a particular target brand and job role.

Then you drive your sales process through an inbound content strategy or outbound telesales or partner with an intermediary to help you find leads.

There are always elements from the 30/30/30/10 in this approach, often method three is combined with method two.

Method three should also sharpen your focus on your Agency positioning, messaging and marketing literature.

Client lead source audit

The first step we would recommend you take is to look at your top 10 or 20 client's spending with you for the past two years. Using each of the three methods, understand where you are getting your originating leads from.

Then using method one, the 30/30/30/10, benchmark where your leads are actually coming from. Identify the areas where you can see an opportunity to unlock even more leads. This is always a great exercise to do.

Personally, we find that method two and three have a longer sales cycle, and usually provide a lower marketing return on investment. Our recommendation would be to adopt all three of the routes outlined above.

THE ONE PERCENT

Account Managers and Client Service Teams are integral to any Agency.

Their role is to 'own' the client relationship, run the client communication, help drive their client's business forward and by offering proactive advice. If these jobs are successfully carried out, then Agency/client revenue increases.

Account Managers should be close to their client's business.

It's imperative that Account Managers are fully up to speed with their clients, and their competitor's, business strategies. As well as with sector knowledge and expertise, trends and innovations in their spaces.

Do your Account Managers use your client's products, could they spend time getting closer to your clients?

How could they get even closer? Could they sell their products for a day, work in their stores, shop in their locations - you get the gist?

Account Managers must understand there are four client buyer types:

The price, value and relationship buyers are all hopefully self-explanatory, you ideally want fewer price and more value and relationship buyers as clients because they are going to trust you more and they understand the added value you offer them, rather than haggling over every quote for an hours work.

Then you have the clients in Agencies who pretend to be a value or a relationships buyer, but in fact are hiding the fact they are actually price buyers. They ask for all the extras then refuse to pay for them. So watch out!

And there are typically four types of client behaviours we have identified over the years. Feel free to create your own types too.

Fame clients

Fame clients want you to help them look good in their job. Agencies should work hard to help them. Help them enter awards for the work you do with them. Plan each piece of work to be something that could be potentially entered into an award.

Fame clients want you to:

- Help them win personal awards.

- Help them win awards for mutual work.

- Help them achieve internal recognition.

- Praise them to their superiors.

- Help them achieve success in their role.

- Buy them a copy of the awards you win together.

Schmooze clients

A Schmooze client wants you to enjoy their working relationship with you. It's not all about 'the work, the work, the work', it's about the Agency/client experience.

Client meetings should be held in more creative locations, Saatchi and Saatchi for example allegedly build their business on lunches and dinner. They must have had a lot of Schmooze clients.

Schmooze clients

- Would rather have meeting over lunch or dinner.

- Like being made a fuss of.

Schmooze clients want you to:

- Always remember their birthdays.

- Run your events in fun locations.

- Make sure client experiences are fun.

- Know their hobbies and interests.

Perfectionist client

THE PERFECTIONIST

The Perfectionist client wants you to make their life simple by just getting things right. They want to look good in their job for a variety of reasons, but mainly because you make their life simple by getting things right.

The Perfectionist rarely cares about awards or the social side of Agencies, they just want the work to be right.

They also care about the details of any work, they will drill down on detail, have processes they want followed.

Perfectionist clients can be found with procurement, and Project Managers as well as more detailed marketing manager or technical manager types.

Perfectionist clients want you to:

- Keep an eye on the detail.

- Never submit a typo.

- Always work to a deadline.

- Always be on budget.

- Never submit bland work.

- Take detailed notes.

- Always be punctual with communications.

Bully client

THE BULLY

The Bully client always wants to tell you how to do your job better. They want more control over you and your performance and want you to always go one step beyond their expectations. The Bully client is emotional, they shout and will be very demanding and testing at times, expecting you to work long hours on their terms to resolve any issues.

They can be also incredibly loyal, although they won't seem it, it's very hard to resign a Bully client account.

Bully clients:

- Shout in meetings and on phone calls.

- Demand you work late nights or weekends.

- Put your ideas down.

- Are the most loyal type.

Bully clients want you to:

- Always be one step ahead of them.

- Never take it personally.

- Make them pay for the service levels they expect.

The earlier your account teams understand which type of client they are dealing with, the more they will be successful. It's vital when pitching for new business, that wherever possible you involve Account Managers because it will enable the client to build a relationship with them from the outset.

It's easy for Account Managers to get caught up in the managing part, reacting to your client's every demand, or getting overly involved in the delivery of their service.

We are embarrassed to say that it took us nine years to get proactive account management working in our Agency. We regularly reacted to our clients' demands and our clients rarely became account-based (growing their investment with us), even when they were retained, consequently the retainers stayed at the same value 95% of the time.

It took us ages to understand that a great relationship leads to great work, it's not just about doing a great job. The closer our relationships became, the better the briefs we got from clients and the more they wanted to hear our ideas and embrace them openly.

For this reason, Account Directors and Managers should be 75% proactive, focusing on managing those client relationships really well, by being one step ahead in terms of strategic ideas, to help grow their accounts.

We appreciate that in the early stages of an Agency you may have no choice but to undertake multiple roles as both Project Manager and Account Manager. But as soon as it is financially viable to hire separate people for these roles, do it. It is absolutely crucial to free up your client facing roles.

That said, it isn't just new or small Agencies who get it wrong, larger established Agencies are also guilty of failing to define the Account Manager role appropriately. We have seen this time and time again with the many Agencies with whom we have worked. How do your Account Manager job descriptions measure up to ours?

An Account Manager should:

1. Communicate client expectations clearly and communicate work back to the clients in a timely and effective manner.

2. Organise regular review meetings through weekly, monthly, quarterly and project-end reviews.

3. Understand the different client types. Tailor the client experience based on which type they are.

4. Keep an up to date CRM database of new business opportunities - also use that CRM to know more about clients' personal and professional interests.

5. Build organisational charts of clients' teams to identify other budget holder roles which may also be able to provide a service too.

6. Work with a wider team to proactively create new ideas for new projects, whether they have a planning background or not.

7. Work hard to build even closer, trusted relationships with clients and deliver a first class client experience.

8. Use surveys or systems like Net Promoter Score to drive client satisfaction. A happy client creates a happy Agency. Everyone's a winner.

9. To conclude, while 99% of Agencies we visit react to clients on the whole, make sure that you are the 1% who follow the eight points above and who take client services to another level; Sure it's tough to find the time (and no one ever really has time), however it's actually not really the time that matters so much as making sure that relationship priorities are aligned from the start.

Ensure that the time that you do take is spent working on what is important, which may not always seem to match what is urgent.

We wanted to finish this section by sharing a few ideas that we've developed over the years, based on our encounters with the most successful Account Managers.

1. Re-pitch to clients every year - give them the same service a new prospective client would receive.

2. Celebrate anniversaries - Do you know the anniversary of all of your clients. Lunches/Drinks/Other? Build on the friendships, the relationships; get closer, it's vital!

3. Enter the clients themselves for awards, not just their work!

4. Make clients look good in your company/then they will help you look good. When a client thanks you, get them to ring up your MD and tell him too.

5. Leverage - favours for favours or leads/referrers/ award entries/testimonials.

To pitch or not to pitch

To Pitch or not to Pitch, that is the question. So firstly, there is a strong divide on this subject. It's almost like a religious divide and so are slightly fearful of declaring our position on the matter knowing we will incur wrath and disapproval from some. But hey, we'll do it anyway.

Our advice is to take both approaches. Not one or the other. We've seen Agencies fail, yes fail, because they adopted a stance on never pitching. And we've seen Agencies fail because they invested too much time and money on pitching. We've also seen Agencies quote and create proposals, not realising they are in a competitive pitch process.

We wouldn't turn down all competitive pitches. We would aim to find as many new business leads as we could. So we would then have a choice, to either pitch competitively or to only accept those opportunities where there were no other Agencies competing for the work.

Most Agencies who moan about the pitch process are usually doing so because they are failing to follow the sales process correctly.

Qualify pitches, and you'll be more successful, more strategic and have twice as many opportunities.

A short (true) story:

When we had our Agency Bluhalo we had a competitor who was local to us, and another a little further away.

Once we started our consulting practice, we worked with both these Agencies.

When we asked the first competitor about a pitch that we knew we won against them, he asked 'What pitch?" He never knew that the new business opportunity in question was even a pitch, let alone that we were competing against him. This is why he lost. It was poor qualification and an inadequate sales process.

The second client knew they were pitching against others but were unaware who they were pitching against. We were aware of him. He turned up with a pen and paper; our team turned up with a full pitch presentation.

We won both pitches.

At an event we were at once, a small Agency approached us and said, "But I never get asked to pitch!".

It then clicked, some people respond to proposals or quote requests, by emailing back a proposal.

We heard a story the other day about one of our clients who was told they had just won a £3m pitch simply by standing up! While the rest of the competition had sat around the table, our client showed the prospect that they had energy and wanted to win the business.

After all, your body language is different when you sit and when you stand, right? Whether you believe in pitching or not, always present to new business opportunities in a way that makes it clear that you really want to work with them.

There were times when we felt competitive pitches were not an option for us. Only recently we were reminded of this when visiting a new client. He explained that a few years ago he tried to pass a lead to us, because at the time the opportunity was too big for him.

He told us he was amazed by our response.

Them - "Hello, we have an opportunity for a £100,000 digital project."

Us - "Will there be others pitching?"

Them - "Yes."

Us - "We're sorry, but we have too many opportunities right now where we have no competition."

The Agency owner told us he was gobsmacked at our response to such a large opportunity.

If your pipeline has more opportunities than you can deliver, you will always be able to put yourself in a position to choose which opportunities to go after or to not have to pitch for. This is why lead generation is so important; the knock on effect of a large pipeline to the rest of your business will be more positive if you get this right.

Here's the challenge for most Agencies with a no-pitch approach.

"Hello, it's Tesla here, we would like you to pitch for our work?"

Your response "Sorry we don't pitch."

Seriously? We get it. Some people would rather walk away, personally we would first qualify the Tesla lead further to understand what our odds of winning might be. See our section on qualification for more information.

Sometimes you need to inject some new business fun/life into the studio, even when the odds of winning are low. You'll be telling all your friends and clients you've been asked to pitch for Tesla, and it will create a great vibe in your Agency. It will also be an excellent experience for all and probably force you to up your pitching game, which will help you on future pitches.

We have all been in the position where we have invested lots of time and energy into a pitch and things haven't gone our way, yet we've always learnt more about ourselves, and the process, along the way. We've built relationships, and we've even returned and won that client back at a later stage.

CHEMISTRY AND CREDS

Firstly, we would ask you to start by creating case studies, and joint case studies, with strategic partners to explain the projects and services you have delivered.

Case Studies are usually structured like this:

1. Challenge/problem to solve.

2. The Idea or Solution.

3. The Results.

4. Client Testimonial.

Create case studies using video format. Then you can adapt the content for all other channels. This structured approach to creating case studies, gives you not only the content for case studies, but you will be able to then slice up the video content easily to create content for award entries and testimonials to go into your new business proposals and presentations.

As we wrote earlier, to sell service we need to build trust and chemistry; we need to demonstrate capability through our documentation.

Chemistry literature was more about our values and having researched the brand to find some strong commonalities.

Credentials (or Creds for short) presentations contain content on who your Agency is, what you do, why you do it, what work you have done for other companies, how you approach your work, how you can help the person you are presenting to and why you understand their business better than anyone else they'll speak to!

When you are invited to more formal, or professionally run, pitch processes, chemistry and credential meetings are more common, however sometimes they are combined meetings where you need to present both. In fact our advice is always take both presentations, just in case you get asked for the other or they are expecting both.

Additionally, for first stage encounters we recommend creating a document called a Statement of Capability, to demonstrate more professionalism. Some Agencies have a simple 'one-pager' - something that could either be left behind with clients or emailed - to give clients a greater insight into what we do; a document that could be easily shared with their colleagues.

When pitching there are always four things to consider concerning documentation:

1. A detailed response to their written brief. (This will be quite detailed).

2. A presentation demonstrating to them that you understand their brief, followed by your proposal; including your ideas and your solutions (this should connect with them visually, emotionally).

3. Try to bring in a kinaesthetic element as well to any pitch, start by always physically printing out any creative design, create where you can, interactive elements and prototypes. These tangible items that can be touched, looked at, interacted with and passed around in a meeting or pitch will always demonstrate extra effort and appeal to those clients who prefer to interact.

We want to stress that the creation of physical pitch assets is a secret weapon. Not only does it help in the pitch itself, but also it really can help post pitch. The amount of times we have heard stories of Agencies winning pitches because the pitch assets were physical items, and as they were left visible in the prospect's offices for the all the wider team at the prospects to see and praise. You may just increase your odds of winning by taking this approach.

As a side note, if you are to leave material behind, using recycled materials is always a must.

4. Pitch theatre; what we mean is something on the pitch that would make us more memorable, sometimes it would be very subtle, occasionally playful. Context is key here. It could be as simple as bringing healthy snacks for a post lunch pitch with a fitness company; creating video interviews with their target audience; through to bringing a live band into a pitch playing a song that brings the destination marketing pitch alive. Making the effort to be innovative or creative should score extra points with clients, as it shows how much you want the work and helps build the emotional connection you need with your prospect.

Finally it's important to save some work for your post pitch strategy, sending in additional information about working together/further ideas/research/findings. All these things help you continue the conversation with the prospect and help you demonstrate you want the business, rather than sitting back just waiting for a decision.

We will talk about the qualification process/documents later in this chapter.

THE COBBLER'S SHOES

As first mentioned in our section The Agency Sales Team, the Marketing Manager for the Agency is ultimately responsible for the Agency lead generation. At Bluhalo, a role we actually recruited by accident, turned out to be one of our biggest successes.

A woman who applied for an Account Manager job with us, had a marketing degree and a background in sales. When we asked why she wanted to be an Account Manager rather than working in marketing she replied that no one would give her the opportunity to do marketing. We asked her to put together a marketing plan for our Agency. When she did so, we were so impressed we recruited her in a marketing role

One of our most significant surprises at Cactus, when we started to advise Agencies, was their lack of a Marketing Manager, and when there was one in place, they tended to be overrun with client work.

There is an old English saying:

"You can always tell a cobbler by his shoes".
Years ago a typical cobbler would wear shoes badly in need of repair, the soles and heels so worn down that he looked to be literally "down at heel".

In other words cobblers spent so much time repairing other people's shoes that they couldn't afford the time to fix their own.

The irony that many Agencies providing marketing services don't have a Marketing Manager was almost comical. 100% a case of the cobbler's shoes.

Our most prominent growth hack if you like has been putting in Marketing Managers, sharing with them our new business methodologies, and transforming how Agencies get their new business leads.

Getting that right leads to better quality work, at better prices, and a likelihood of having to do less pitching. It's an investment hire that if you get right will transform your Agency.

Marketing Managers also help with:

1. Client retention

- Source events for clients to attend.

- Client events.

- Assists with client communication.

- Client awards.

- Net Promoter Score.

2. Partnerships

- Maximise partnerships by reviewing joint case studies.

- Liaise with partners over upcoming opportunities.

- Create events with partners.

- Ensure partners see the value in your relationship.

- Identify more partnerships.

3. Networking (socialising & speaking)

- Identify a calendar of events for founders to attend.

- Source events which give access to big clients and specific sectors.

- Create company documents based on 'thought leadership'.

- Help build Director's and team's profiles to help identify and source speaking opportunities.

4. Content marketing

- Assists with PR.

- Manages social media and community management.

- Creates marketing communications such as email and other communication pieces.

- Marketing Managers will be tenacious; 90% hands on, 10% strategic and building up momentum in gaining new business opportunities.

- Will act as an extra resource in your team and will always pay for themselves, even if you can't charge them out to a client.

Marketing budget

Typically you should reinvest 7.5-10% of your gross profit into marketing, or 5% while also employing a full-time Marketing Manager.

When should you recruit a full-time Marketing Manager?

We would recommend making this appointment if your company has a turnover of above £750,000 (sooner if you have the cash to invest in the role). If you are sub £900,000, and don't have the budget to recruit, try to get part-time help.

If you do opt for part-time help, our recommendation is to try to get a specialist to help in each area, e.g. don't hire one person to do it all. Get one person to help run events, another person to write your case studies, etc. you'll get more traction this way.

To be clear, when hiring a Marketing Manager in an Agency you need to find someone who is highly organised, probably 90% hands on and 10% strategic. Someone who has holistic marketing experience of working in a services business and can demonstrate experience of organising events, good at finding speakers and socialising opportunities, as well as forming strategic partnerships and curating content.

MIND MAPPING

As we've already identified in the Agency New Business methodologies section of this book, 90% of Agency leads come from the 30/30/30 areas.

In the next three sections we will cover these areas in more detail and also talk about building fame. But first, let's talk about the importance of socialising and speaking.

We think this says it all:

Spencer's socialising story

Six weeks into starting my Agency, freshly armed with business cards, I borrowed a car and drove down to Brighton, on the south coast of the UK, to do some research for a potential client brief.

I grabbed a cup of tea at the end of the conference and asked the event speaker the question I needed to. Suddenly an elderly gentleman, who happened to be an accountant, approached me and asked me what I did, I replied, and he told me that he thought that websites could be the future for business and took a card. Pretty smart accountant.

Two weeks later, I randomly got a phone call from someone in London, who had been given a card by his accountant who was based in Brighton! My first ever business card went on to win one of my first projects, building a website for the Talent Management Agent of the 90's dance band Orbital, my first music/artist related client.

Yet it took me six years to realise the value socialising had brought to my new business wins, or maybe I was just in denial.

Socialising was a love-hate relationship for me. I loved meeting people who shared my growth mindset, values and passion for tech, but often I would be surrounded by people who I didn't connect to. Six years in I started to fully realise the value socialising brought the business.

I cut my teeth on some horrible, small business networking gigs but, for all my moaning, they taught me valuable lessons. I mastered my craft and gained invaluable experience, which as my networks grew I could take with me. But let's not knock these events, I still find deals from major brands who originated in some of the smallest businesses growth networks there are.

Sure, there was serendipity to the socialising, and yes, sometimes, the harder I worked at it the luckier I got; at other times it would feel like wasted time and investment.

But as the familiar meme says, one of the most significant asset investments you can make in life is in your network of connections.

Success in life has an element of what you know and who you know doesn't it? For some people networking and building business connections is a no-go area. Well if that's the case for you, you'll need to hope that your business partner does.

The network you build can take years to develop, and if you hand it over to a member of your team to do on your behalf, you will find that when they leave, the network they have built will go with them, and your business will lose the value.

The key is to take a different approach and mindset to the challenge of building a great set of personal and business connections, which is why I call it socialising.

It's funny, seven years after I sold Bluhalo I referred-in a £500,000 opportunity to one of my Agency clients with two deals that had come from someone I met seven years prior to when I had my business. Did I mention B2B sales has a long sales cycle? Socialising, done correctly, keeps on giving for years to come.

Firstly, we should ban the word networking from Agency life; it often conjures up the wrong images. Let's keep calling it building business contacts, connections or even just socialising!

Next, with our new approach committed to making exciting new business connections, let's make a list of the things you enjoy doing and let's see how we could combine meeting people with common shared interests.

When I've run new business masterclasses with brands, they are always saying how they want to meet people with shared interests. One such person, a business owner declared that he was into kitesurfing, and that if he was invited to an event which involved this activity, he would be highly likely to attend.

Many people share stories with me about how they met their Agency or client through experiences like:

- Triathlons.

- Cycling.

- Golf.

- Holiday Locations

- Their children's School.

- Neighbours,

- Shared car journeys.

- Beer tasting.

- Paddle boarding

- Hot Yoga.

- Cooking lessons

Business relationships are found everywhere; it's worth remembering that if you are genuinely interested in people *and* business, the two will authentically create connections and opportunities for you.

Of course, particular interests attract different levels of seniority, no question that a lot of CEOs, CMOs and CIO like their cycling and triathlons.

Many Agencies and industry trade bodies run cycling events for many, offering the chance to combine social and business interests, which makes it all worthwhile.

That said, there are also some unusual events which bring together people in your sector. Keep an eye out for these events and once there, look for the people you want to work with, find your common interests and a way to bring learn+play or work and play together.

Use your imagination.

For me, the sector I was most excited about was sports. I was helped by the persona work we did on our own and target clients in 2005, where all the clients were into one sport or another.

Let's be clear I'm not an obsessive sports nut, I like a couple of sports, but I liked the industry a lot more. I loved the way digital was impacting on this area through the 2000's and started to go to all events that targeted people working in sports marketing.

Over the following three years we built some significant relationships. Not everyone went on to work with me, but it made the world smaller knowing all the people in that sector, someone always knew someone.

Before we knew it, we were the largest bespoke builder of digital projects in the sports area, and we had become a sort of 'go-to' Agency for all things digital, sport and fan engagement.

If you have ever heard one of my talks, you'll know I'm a massive fan of only having one Key Performance Indicator (KPI) in your Agency, the number people you meet monthly.

My target started at trying to meet 15 new connections a month and rose to 50 new connections a month. That focus enabled me to drive in over £200,000 of new business every month. Of course every person has their number, but there was a correlation between the relevant (and sometimes less relevant) people I met, and new business opportunities. And of course, over time, you learn to connect with more senior people who are more relevant to your journey.

Eventually, you hit a tipping point, which for me was around 1500 connections. Three years in on LinkedIn I had met or spoken to everyone I had connected to in person; as a result, inbound opportunities would start to flow frequently.

It's easy today to collect large numbers of connections on social media but try to make sure you aim for connections who you have actually met or spoken to in real life and well you actually like them. Those contacts on the whole will carry more value and are likely to drive more leads and referrals than those who you have not met.

Consider Mind Mapping your connections with key contacts like this example.

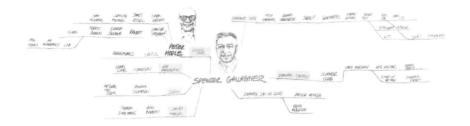

Mind Mapping helped remind us of those people who were the super-connectors in our network. Super connectors would keep referring us to people who would want to work with us.

It also helped us identify the people who maybe we spent too much time with, those who offered little or no opportunity, but perhaps added value in other ways.

In this section we want to share our best socialising tips. We always tell people who are happy to network, and those who are not, to master their craft, invest time in learning how to socialise. We aren't talking about being inauthentic or fake. In our experience, those who describe networking or socialising in such a way are simply using it as their excuse to not have to do it.

Firstly it's important to meet people and genuinely feel a connection. It won't happen to everyone, some people you meet you will just not connect with, others you will.

Usually, there will be some social proof, a common interest or the like, which allows you to learn more about each other. The most important thing when socialising is to listen to others, ask about their interests and be genuine. If you don't like them, then be polite and then go meet someone else; and when you do connect, listen as much as possible and try to help that person in some way.

It's widely agreed that the most successful people are givers, so when building business contacts, try to listen and help people, develop a strong chemistry and a trusted relationship.

Don't force what you do on others and work hard to communicate what you do in less than ten words, so that people are clear about what you do and how you help others.

For Spencer, back in the day, it was always "If you ever meet anyone who needs help developing a website or has a digital project, here's my card, please feel free to pass it on," or "I'm always happy to help people by giving them advice for free or connecting them to someone else who can help."

That line never sold to people directly, but they would often then say, "I want your help!" But we later learnt it is called a 'future trigger point' because, although when we used that line most people did not yet have websites, when they went on to meet someone in the coming months who did need us, we were often referred work. The introductions were relentless at times.

We have heard a lot about business referrals being poor quality; that's simply not true. Of course, when you start you get a lot of the same small business clients referring other small businesses.

But as your clients and your network grow in seniority, the referral quality grows too; people like to refer people like themselves.

Public speaking

It's funny, we always viewed speaking events as a social opportunity to get to meet more people in one go! You know, we'd go to a networking event and meet maybe five people, yet if we spoke at an event, at the end of the event at least 10 people from the audience would then approach whoever was speaking that day.

The more of your wider team who can speak at events, the better! We have a client with a team of 30 and at least a quarter of the team are capable of speaking at events.

Speaking builds trust on many levels. As an expert, you get to demonstrate chemistry and credentials in one go. It qualifies those people in the audience who need to speak to you, and those who don't. Over the past 20 years we have seen some of the best opportunities coming from speaking events, yet many Agency owners haven't embraced this.

Sure there are cases where a fear of public speaking gets in the way, and we once had to get a friend to hypnotise three Directors who all had a fear of speaking. You have to give them credit for recognising the importance of speaking and being open enough to try overcoming their fear.

Finding speaking events is tough at first because you need to build up your expert status, then visit a lot of events, connect with the organisers and pitch to them why your talks would add value to their events.

We try to have two or three talks, one about our service specialisms/future trends and one about the business itself: the culture, overcoming challenges and things we felt we did differently to other businesses. This gave us the flexibility to speak to broader audiences from business owners and entrepreneurs of all sizes, through to sector specialists.

We want to emphasise the importance of speaking and holding panel events by giving you an example. One panel event we organised, advising people on how to scale their businesses, generated over £300,000 worth of business. We cannot share enough stories where speaking has driven in significant new business leads. We always remember how an Agency owner friend told us that the lead for her top client, a global car manufacturer, came from an event she spoke at.

Another was someone we once met at a dinner whose Agency had hit £500,000 in its first year, and whose clients include major brands. We asked him how he was marketing his Agency and he said that in month one he had spoken at an event and won some business. He then decided that he should speak more frequently, sometimes as often as twice a month, at similar events where the audience could be potential clients for him.

Today we speak at a lot of events, but it wasn't always like that. It started with us talking to a small team, and then over time speaking to a larger team of 20 or 30 and now we have audience of over 100. It's a journey full of learning, with plenty of resources and training on offer to help master this craft.

If you crack it, you'll get to that magic figure of 50 new business connections a month and generate many more leads for your business.

FRENEMIES & MORE

Another significant way to generate new business leads is from the strategic partnership and alliances you put in place with other complementary organisations.

Some examples of strategic partnerships could be with your key clients, whereby you contra all or some of your Agency services in exchange for introductions or referrals from your client.

A good example of this is when we had our Agency, two of our clients became strategic partners. Our partnerships with both Tottenham Hotspur and Subaru not only saw us working for both clients on a paid basis, but we agreed to contra some services in an exchange of value. For example, The Subaru World Rally Team (SWRT), gave us access to meet other sponsors of the club through exclusive socialising and introductions as well as track days and other premium hospitality.

One of the most common partnerships we come across today are with technology partners. At Bluhalo it was our partnership with NTT Communications, one of the world's largest communication brands that had the biggest impact on our Agency's success.

Our strategic partnership with NTT, was of significant mutual benefit at the time. We needed their technology to host larger digital properties, and they couldn't host those properties without a web application being built first.

NTT's network had a huge sports focus with flagship clients like UEFA Champions League, which helped us expand our social connections in the sports sector; and it seemed almost overnight our pipeline started to bring in a whole array of opportunities for new clients. With NTT's network and help, we were able to pitch for clients such as Manchester City FC and we went on to win a whole host of sports clients over the following few years.

In addition, we were able to leverage their sponsorship partnership with The Champions League and extend this hospitality to our clients. We, in turn, helped NTT break into some of the other sectors, like e-Commerce, which we were particularly skilled at. We were also able to help them create a selection of Agency Partners, to expand their business into other sectors.

Lots of large tech brands; Google, Microsoft, Facebook, Amazon, make good Agency partners. It's quite common to see Content Management System (CMS) vendors, as well as sector-specific applications, like Magento, WordPress, Microsoft Cognitive Services. In addition, for those whose Agencies have more of a design, branding or creative approach, partnerships with large printers, paper stock manufacturers, other creative material suppliers can also provide key strategic partnerships.

Complementary Agencies also provide a secure partner network. These are the most common type of partnership we come across in the early days of Agency life. When you are a smaller Agency, help can come from being outsourced partners of larger Agencies, but the key here is to be introduced from the outset as a partner so that you can retain the value in owning the client relationship and receive credit for the work done publicly.

As you grow, you will begin to work side by side with larger brands who often like to work with best in breed Agencies. Your ability to demonstrate your skills to a partner will serve you well. In the early years, outsourced projects can give you the confidence to demonstrate you are capable of working on such brands.

Your Agency suppliers are often overlooked as potential partners. It's essential you understand that if you buy from suppliers on price, so be it. But if you buy them for the value they add, then you need to know what that value is, and how they can help you. We also want to say that we believe that only people who know how to *buy* on value, can typically *sell* value.

We always use the NTT examples here, because before partnering with NTT, a premium more enterprise hosting company, we hosted with a low-cost hosting provider.

The low-cost provider never added any value to our Agency business other than as a cheap, reliable service; which for many would be great, especially the techies in your team. However, it was the switch to NTT that, through working together, added value back in so many ways.

We would always provide NTT with help for their case studies and make ourselves available for references. We would spend time with their team and they would spend time with ours. They would educate us on the areas we didn't know a lot about; in turn we would promote them to our clients. A strategic alliance with such a large organisation as NTT also helped our service offering to be much more credible.

Ask yourself, who are your suppliers? How could they add value to your Agency? Ask yourself if your printing service, accountant, lawyer, bank or consultants could add value if you gave them a chance to do so. Other suppliers are often business owners too, with their own networks. So seek to see if you could help each other by adding more value beyond the initial service that they provided you with.

Media organisations can also help create strategic partnerships as you can help them create content in exchange for them helping you with the distribution of that content.

For example, you could help a sector trade publication by providing them with unique content of value. Or perhaps offer something along the lines of let's say, "a sector survey" in exchange for their promoting the survey and then the results exclusively and allowing you access to meet people within this sector.

Finally, partnerships can come from sponsorships because sometimes sponsorship provides you with a way to access markets for your target sectors. A sponsorship might, for example, enable you to get access to an event where Agencies may not usually be allowed to attend.

WHEN WILL I BE FAMOUS

One way to boost sales as an Agency is by achieving industry fame or notoriety.

If your Agency is celebrated as a market leader, it naturally generates new business for you.

Certain C-level Execs with big budgets will prefer to work with famous Agencies due to their market reputation.

A big name Agency with a successful awards track record, provides security for the people working at larger Brands, as those Agencies are seen as a safe pair of hands.

Not only this, but a famous Agency is more attractive and desirable for brands to use, because they can use their association with the Agency to improve their own status and build their own personal fame and reputation.

There is almost a celebrity factor with these Agencies, the most prominent probably being the likes of Saatchi & Saatchi. For example, it's best to have a well-known actor starring in your film rather than an unknown actor who could pose a risk.

Every Agency likes to receive recognition for the work it creates. It is rewarding to be recognised for good work, and fame tends to bring with it some value-added benefits.

For example:

- You'll start to attract and retain the best talent.

- Other prospective clients like to be associated with successful Agencies.

- It keeps you in front of your intermediaries mind.

- Fame simply creates more fame, suddenly everything in your Agency becomes a little more newsworthy.

- It increases your Agency and teams' credibility.

- You'll find your Agency will be invited into other pitches or asked to quote for new work.

Achieving fame also gives you and your Agency:

- More confidence and self-belief.

- More opportunities to pitch.

- The ability to win more awards.

- Increase journalistic interest.

- Greater perceived trust in your abilities.

- An increase in your pitch win rate.

- Respect from your industry peers.

The first consideration for you to figure out is what it is that you want to be famous for. Once you have done this put the following steps in place:

- Create a separate "Fame Budget" 2 to 3% of GP.

- Set some goals and make a plan.

- Build fame into the brief: "What's the press release?".

- Get the whole Agency involved in promoting any fame projects.

- Drive word of mouth – establish three key things about your Agency that everyone can talk about.

- Don't wait for the perfect brief, create your own internal projects that you could use for fame.

Make sure you release internal fame projects:

- Internal projects can be the most challenging.

- Don't allow them to drag on.

- Have a tight brief and stick to it.

- Manage internal stakeholders – try not to have too many cooks.

- Accept it won't be perfect. DON'T endlessly tweak it.

- Get it out there and move on!

Create a fame plan:

- Create a content calendar for the next 12 month.

- Assign responsibility for each strand to the people in your team.

- Appraise them on performance in these areas.

- Working as a management team, review your "fame forecast" monthly.

- Manage resources carefully - back the winners.

Five things you could start doing today:

1. Plan a "big idea" event which supports your proposition.

2. Brainstorm a headline grabbing stunt with the entire Agency.

3. Approach three famous conferences and pitch for speaking opportunities.

4. Write the brief for a fame project, either adding to an existing client brief or by creating an internal fame project to be released externally.

5. Scour the press, cut out and storyboard other similar Agency stories that you could have submitted. Then create your own versions of the stories adding a twist or two where you can.

COMPETITIVE INTELLIGENCE

We first heard the words 'competitive intelligence' when we went to a talk on the subject, at around the time our Agency turnover was £500,000.

Our feeling at that time was that as we didn't have any particular competitors and we certainly never pitched against the same company twice, the talk seemed totally irrelevant for us. Since then we've certainly learnt that as your Agency grows, or as you start to focus on your service proposition, you suddenly start to find the same competitors arising time and time again. The point we are trying to make here is that things can change quickly, so if you don't feel you have key competitors right now, this may change anytime soon.

For us it came less than two years after that talk we went to. Suddenly we had become one of the largest Agencies in the region and were starting to be recognised as an Agency player in the sports sector

We won a particular pitch with a company who then shared with us the competitor's pitch documents. We were so shocked; we couldn't believe how much people were charging! And we couldn't believe the packaging for the proposals created: beautifully designed boxes, USB drives, large printed & mounted storyboards (even for digital work) and the videos they'd put together!

It was a rude awakening for us as we realised we needed to up our game; sure we had won the pitch and our work was strong, but there was still a lot of great packaging around our competitor's pitch assets.

We then lost a pitch to one of our competitors and our whole team felt determined not to be beaten by them again. We cheekily asked the client for a copy of the competing pitch and, once we had this intelligence, the next time we managed to beat those competitors. We never lost to them again.

The next section talks about the importance of qualification, and how one of the questions you should be asking yourself is, "How much do we understand about who we are pitching against?". The more competitive intelligence you get, the more you will understand how to beat your competitors.

As we've stated many a time, the best Agencies don't win pitches, it's the ones who know how to pitch to win against their competitors. We've been the best Agency and lost pitches, and, if we are really honest about it, a few other times we've won pitches against stronger candidates.

Understanding your competition is less about whether you are likely to beat the competition, face them in a pitch, or even care about who their clients are. It's more about the learning that such an understanding brings.

For example we set up a dinner for Agency founders with the sole purpose of making friends with other Agency owners. Our intention was not to talk about their clients, or new business, but to share some empathy about the way an Agency is run. We love how collaborative 95% of Agency owners are compared with other industries. We are a giving industry, and we love seeing the knowledge sharing and collaboration that comes out of keeping your friends close and your enemies closer!

Here follows a story which we've recently been quoting a lot, especially after reading some negative comments about how disingenuous socialising with competitors can be.

Our client, let's call him Alex, was on a pitch for a £300,000 piece of work, and we asked who he was competing with. Alex rolled off the competitors' names, one of whom is an Agency known to us as a strong competitor, as well as a great Agency.

Alex had told us he'd met the owner of this particular Agency a year ago, when they were both at much smaller networking events, and they had become friends.

Once they knew they were competing against each other, they spoke and wished each other good luck. One week later the other Agency rang Alex and said the prospect didn't want their technology of choice for the solution but they wanted Alex's preferred technology framework.

The other Agency had made it very clear to the prospect that he knew Alex well, and that if the prospect wanted to take the technology route, then he should 100% choose them. We can only imagine just what the prospect must have thought of an Agency verbally praising another, with whom he was in direct competition, with such enthusiasm.

So, if you are one of the 5% of Agencies who don't believe in socialising with competitors, try telling us now that it's not worth it!

We have a good few dozen of these stories if you ever want to have a beer and debate sometime.

Of course, there is a line. We wouldn't want to spend more than 20% of our socialising time with other Agencies, but by connecting with them from time-to-time you will get more value, and more good advice than you could ever afford to buy.

#FFFF

Qualification, or qualifying an opportunity, is one of the things we'd most like you to understand and work on in your Agency. For along with Sales and Finance, Qualification is one of the most misunderstood parts of the sales process within an Agency.

Qualifying an opportunity properly can give you a sense of whether the deal is worth pitching for or not, and this can save you time, money and effort – enabling you to focus on only the opportunities that you have the greatest chance of winning.

There are arguably three ways to qualify an opportunity:

1. Some use the Fun, Fame, Fortune criteria. Will it be fun to work on? Will it bring us fame? Will it make us a fortune? (Well, provide a solid commercial opportunity for the Agency at least).

2. One client cleverly added 'forward' to this criteria, as in, 'will this opportunity take us forward? to make it the "FFFF" of qualification?'

3. Then there's the "what's your budget?" question. A speedy way to establish qualification is via asking for their budget. Of course if a client's budget is less than a certain amount then you are well within your rights to say no. You may have decided to only take on projects over £15,000.

But of course, use common sense as well. There are always exceptions. For example, if a recognised brand came to you with a budget of £10,000, it would not always be sensible to say no if you were to see an opportunity of this big brand investing more with you next time.

It's also important to point out that with today's more agile approach to business, it's becoming more common to see initial smaller trial budgets, where a client may want to run some kind of discovery or strategy style meeting before leading onto larger projects. In this way, qualifying out a small opportunity should be approached with caution because you don't know what it will lead to.

Using a qualification scoring system so you could score the opportunity holistically. Let us explain more:

We love to talk about the game Texas Hold'em because most people believe it's a game of luck, whereas its beauty lies in the fact that it's actually a game of skill. Well we'll argue perhaps a little luck helps, but record-breaking American, Phil Hellmuth hasn't won 15 World Series of Poker bracelets, because he's super lucky has he?

Winning Texas Hold'em depends less on the cards you are dealt, and more on how you choose to play them.

The same applies to Agency leads. It's not so much the leads that you receive that matters, as the ones you decide to go for.

In poker, the odds state that if your starting hand is a pair of aces then you have more than an 80% chance of winning.

If you have a two and a seven off suit then that's a 53% chance.

If you have odds on a lead of 80% and you are likely to win, wouldn't you play the pitching game?

In Agencies, if you ask the right questions, you can start to get a picture of your odds of winning. That doesn't mean you'll win everything, statistically if you have 10 deals of 80% you'll lose two.

Once you know your Agency's odds, maybe the whole no-pitch agenda becomes a little less relevant to you? Or perhaps you feel 80% is still not high enough odds to change your mind?

There are exceptions - we've won a £350,000 deal with just 16% odds. We pitched at such low odds because at the time we felt we had no choice but to pitch as we had few leads.

It's also worth noting that in this particular case we worked out that everyone else pitching had 16% odds, which led us to believe that most of the competition would actually pull out. So in eventuality our odds increased as a result of the competition pulling out.

We've also lost deals with a 100% qualification score too. The odds game is not perfect, but statistically it mostly works.

At Bluhalo our qualification catchphrase was:

"No brief, no budget, no deadline, no deal."

We created the qualification tool we use for Agencies today by accident when we were invited to help solve an Agency's new business problem.

We created a spreadsheet version of our manual qualifying system and asked the client to score their opportunities - they all came back as 43% or less on our scoring system.

We now know from historical data that such a score means they should win just one in twelve deals on average, and that's only an 8% win rate.

The reason their qualification score was so low, was because their leads were coming the lazy way. They pretty much only partnered with Agencies to generate leads for them.

All those Agencies had relationships with the prospects, not our client. The Agency we were helping was pretty much used to providing highly speculative ideas for the other Agencies' clients.

Let's be clear: as an Agency generating up to £1m in revenues, it's going to be a fact of life that some of your business will come from other Agencies outsourcing or partnering with you.

Beware though, if you don't have a direct relationship with the end client, then there will be no real value in the long term.

While these types of deals can fix some short-term sales and cash issues, unless you are partnering side by side (and in most cases owning the sales process with a client), there really will be no long-term value in that relationship.

You won't be able to promote the work either; because the client relationship is owned by the lead Agency, rather than you, you will be unable to enter it for awards or grow the account in any way.

We are sure a few of you have this working nicely, and yes there are always exceptions, but on the whole direct relationships will help you control your Agency pipeline.

We discovered that when this particular Agency received a score of 70% or above, they pretty much always won the deal.

Over time we've taken a snapshot of the win-loss ratios of our client's data, and the numbers seem to work again and again. It's like we've discovered the Fibonacci sequence. Ultimately there is a "numbers game" in play here.

The higher your deals qualify, the more chance you have of winning.

There's one final curveball to throw in when discussing qualifying opportunities.

Ideally, one client should never equate to more than 20% of your turnover and you should be working hard to make this less than 10%. So make sure that this new prospect represents less than 20% of your turnover; if it is more, are you confident you can dilute it back down to a lower percentage fairly quickly in the short term?

If you lose a client account worth 10% of your client base, it may not impact your business too materially. But if you lose a client who represents 20-30% of your turnover, you will almost certainly have to restructure your team size.

When winning larger step-change deals, know that deals that take you up to the next level are part and parcel of Agency life, just always be careful of exposing your business unnecessarily, by always ensuring that the next step change deal is on the horizon.

Also be aware that if you focus your business exclusively in one business sector, you need to try to make sure that you also work in periphery sectors, in case of a downturn in your main sector. Try to ensure that you are working in around four different sectors, until you are confident enough that there is no risk in focusing on one sector as you have a wide enough range of clients in this sector.

Some people believe it is good to be specialists, for example focusing solely on retail or the automotive sectors, as this can generate many big contracts. History once again proves that this is not safe.

The companies who solely focused on automotive or financial services from 2007 to 2009, now know that most car manufacturers and financial institutions had to cut their budgets throughout their organisations due to the global financial crisis. One of our competitors, unfortunately, lost all their customers in just one quarter during this period.

Qualification Score:

Here is an example of our "qual score" document we use daily with clients. If you own, or work in an Agency and would like permission to use this and receive a copy of the Agencynomics qualification score tool we are happy to share it as an interactive Google document, with the results statistics guide. Please email us to request a copy to hello@agencynomics.com

Pitch Qualification Document	Yes = 1 No=0
Client Name:	Acme Ltd
Was there a brief? Or will the client pay for a discovery /strategy session?	1
Was there a budget?	1
Do we have a mole? (or if an existing client – do we have a good client relationship?)	0
Do we know the names of the Agencies we are up against?	1
Are you the only company pitching?	0
Will they meet us face to face pre-pitch (or pre-proposal)?	1
Is there a deadline for the project sign-off or launch?	1
Total % Chance	71%

THINKING AND DOING

When the majority of Agencies start their journey, they take the approach of "Let me do for you," and don't charge for the "Let me think for you," strategy or planning work.

It's often a confidence thing as the majority of Agencies in their early years work with small brands and smaller budgets and get used to not selling the full value of what they do, as there are not the budgets to do so.

The same often happens with project management, it's given away for free in the early days, the habit then remaining as the Agency scales.

As an Agency scales, or if the Agency started out as more of a consultancy, it then moves to the "Let me think for you," and possibly also the "Let me do for you," as well.

This is the shift that we call the selling of value not time; although many people may still sell the "Let me think for you," as time, so without losing the revenue all together though not fully in the 'value' space.

We would urge every one of you to invest in learning more about this area because it will give you a great insight into the difference between time and value. For a list of books devoted to selling value, go to the book list in the back of this book.

Of course, there are businesses out there who will want to sell the time-based "Let me do for you". And as long as they are acutely aware of the potential commoditisation of their services, and have high-quality processes, there is nothing wrong with such a strategy.

When an Agency decides to focus on just the delivery or the strategy, and either splits the business into two or drops one or the other offering, it is sometimes referred to as decoupling.

For example, the "Let me do for you" Agency might say: if you want the value strategy and advice, go elsewhere first, then come back to us when you are ready.

Or

The "Let me think for you" Agency will say: we'll create the strategy, then you go elsewhere for the execution.

For those of you who currently feel you are giving away too many areas of your non-delivery services for free, and are planning a shift to the selling more of those areas please note, it's quite a shift and will take quite a few changes in your approach to make it work.

The first change is to sell the 'thinking' as a service, and to do this you need to recognise all the things that create the extra value in your business delivering those services.

To learn to sell consultancy, you need to focus more on the results and the outcomes of your work, and demonstrate at least a 10x return on investment for your thinking.

Additionally, to sell value you need to have value or relationships buyers, not price buyers. You need buyers who will understand what the impact of working with you over another Agency would be. If you have a price buyer, you will need to qualify these people out unless you have an ingenious way of converting these buyer types, like Don Draper did in the TV series Mad Men.

The key to selling value is to understand the impact of the thinking that you will be doing; people are expecting a 10x return on your advice, so it's vital that you can demonstrate your ability to do this for them. To achieve it you will need a higher level of understanding about your client's business; and you will also need to demonstrate a proven track record, or a process and a case study to demonstrate this.

Value comes from areas such as your experience, the consultant/strategist's expertise and profile, your tried and tested processes and methodologies. It is the amount of time invested in these areas that you are passing forward. It's also the way you position things. Our first experience of this came one day when we met a competitor who told us he had moved his day rate to £1,200 from £800 a day, and no one had quibbled that he was not offering both the thinking and doing services.

When we then won a pitch against this Agency and asked the client for a copy of the competitor's presentation, we saw that the competitor had changed the 'day' rate to 'studio day' rate. It was an example of how wording can carry a perceived value, a studio day rate meaning that up to three people a day will be working on the allocated work rather than one. The point here was that we'd always had two more people adding value in some way to each person's billing, and now we were recovering the thinking and value-added bits that we had been giving away.

Ultimately the client wasn't paying more because at that stage our efficiencies meant that we were delivering more in less time.

Our expertise had been creating a law of diminishing returns. We seemed to be delivering even more work in less time, while paying more for talented team members to do this.

With better quality, more experienced team members delivering work more quickly, with processes improving our speed of delivery, it was time to change our pricing strategy to allow us to charge for our value and skills in delivery.

This saw a win-win for all involved. In fact, the increase in our day rate also meant we could factor in a budget for over-servicing, which kept the clients even happier.

The sooner you understand how to sell both the thinking and the doing, the more you will protect your margins as you scale, and the faster your Agency will succeed.

Chapter 5: Delivering Happiness

PARKINSONS LAW

Managing the delivery process by specialist, dedicated staff is the key to underpinning the growth of any Agency, whether it be through Project Management (PM) or Studio/Operations Management.

For years the traditional advertising and marketing Agency world stuck to the model of client service teams who would deal with delivery and project management, mainly because the organising was relatively straightforward to do.

Agencies used to have a clear line of structure with the Client Service Director at the top, followed by the Account Director, Account Manager, Account Executive and finally a graduate.

This team of account management people would manage their clients and their projects so instead of having a separate Account Manager and Project Manager, the Account Managers would also project manage. Sometimes you would also find Production Managers who would manage third parties, such as print management or event production and from time to time you would see other roles such as Studio Managers who would oversee scheduling.

With the integration of digital technology the Agency landscape needed more dedicated project management expertise.

As technology became more of a driver, through the advertising and marketing Agency, the skills of the account management team were not enough to deliver more complex projects. The convergence of digital Agencies with traditional Agencies helped alleviate this by adding roles such as the project manager, business analyst, producer, or solutions specialist, to the more traditional Agency roles.

These days, for most Agencies, especially where digital is at the heart of everything, it is more commonplace to have Account Management and Project Management as separate roles.

The Agencies that offer pure consultancy services, or have more retained services such as PR, SEO & social media Agencies, still seem to have little or no project management roles. We feel it is crucial that you employ someone who ensures your services are getting managed in line with client's expectations, and preventing your delivery teams from suffering from Parkinson's law.

Parkinson's law is the adage that "Work expands to fill the time available for its completion".

We have also proven time and time again the benefits of having a Project Manager with the right personality traits, will create:

1. A more proactive client service culture. Lack of proactivity is something a large majority of clients cite as their number one complaint against Agencies.

2. A more reliable delivery service with fewer people doing the work, rather than the countless throwing bodies at the solution approach.

The result is that there are more people left to get on and execute great work, freed up from having to deal with clients directly (as there are better people in the Agency to do this now). And service delivery people, now having someone dedicated to support them in delivering their work, can become more efficient. Sounds obvious, doesn't it?

An Agency's attitude to project management has a major impact on Agency growth. It determines whether an Agency will grow quickly or not. Those who see project management as an investment, and the cornerstone of a good business are likely to thrive, whereas those who see it as an unnecessary overhead and/or additional bureaucracy tend to remain in the slow lane.

We go on to talk about project management in greater detail in this chapter, covering the role itself (and other areas such as reporting and methodologies), but we feel the illustration below sums up perfectly why we feel project management is important.

To illustrate the difference project management can make, here's a comparison of three Agencies we worked with. We provided the same service to each and all were at a run rate of £1.5m turnover.

	AGENCY 1	AGENCY 2	AGENCY 3
TURN OVER	£1.5m	£1.5m	£1.5m
STAFF	30	25	20
PROJECT MANAGERS	1	2	3
PROFIT	0%	5%	10%

Agency One had 31 staff, of which only one was a Project Manager. They were extremely inefficient, made no profit, and believed that the way to solve problems around delivery was to throw more bodies at the problem.

Agency Two lay somewhere in the middle. Out of their 27 staff they had two Project Managers , and although they were slightly more efficient, they still had too many fee earners and not enough organisation of the troops.

Agency Three, although on paper seemingly light on staff, were highly efficient as they had three Project Managers organising the team, managing workflows and client expectations.

Projects were rarely late, and rarely over serviced. Since they were the most efficient Agency, they made the most profit, with the least amount of staff delivering the highest fees per employed head.

At the £3m turnover level we had three PM's, who were all in individual pods or teams (we cover pods later in the book).

They also acted as one project management team, with the studio resource being managed very effectively by the three of them. Knowing what we know now and as detailed in the beginning of this chapter, we would probably have four PM's at this stage to drive further efficiency.

The reason for this is that the savings in efficiency would still be considerably greater than the cost of the additional salary.

It's actually very unusual to have an Operations Manager in an Agency under 40 staff. We don't want to go so far as to say that it doesn't work, because if you have several founders, the role may suit one of those individuals.

The PM

The role of the Project Manager is to plan and execute any work an Agency has agreed to undertake.

- They need to understand the defined scope of the project to be undertaken, to plan the start and work towards a defined finish.

- The PM manages the work allocated to the delivery team and supports them with any issues or challenges that arise during the project cycle. They must do everything to ensure successful delivery, including making certain that the project is delivered in line with the expectations, which will be set from the start.

- As we mentioned above, keeping close contact with the team, the expected deliverable and the timeline will help prevent the Parkinson's law situation as referred to earlier in this book.

- The PM helps the team to not get caught up in direct communications with the client, which helps with overall efficiency.

- We recommend that it is the Account Manager who manages client communication. On the whole try to keep the Account Manager managing the client, and the Project Manager managing the team and the project delivery. The exception to this is if the contact at the client is a detail focussed person you may need to swap managing communications from the account team to the project team.

- The PM is accountable for ensuring that everyone on the team knows and executes his or her role, feels empowered and supported in their role, knows the roles of the other team members, and acts upon the belief that those roles will be performed. The specific responsibilities of the PM may vary, depending on the industry, the company size, the company maturity, and the company culture.

  However, there are some responsibilities which are common to all PMs, notably.

- Developing the project plans & managing stakeholders.

- Managing communication.

- Managing the project team.

- Managing the project risk.

- Managing the project schedule.

- Managing the project budget.

- Managing the project conflicts.

- Managing the project delivery.

DON'T GO CHASING WATERFALLS

These are the two most popular forms of delivery methodology and are usually described as follows:

1. Waterfall: which might be more properly called the "traditional" approach, taking from the earlier days of software development, where progress flows in one direction from design, build, testing, deployment and:

2. Agile: a specific type of Rapid Application Development, refers to a group of development methodologies based on iterative development, where requirements and solutions evolve through collaboration between self-organising cross-functional teams.

The Waterfall Methodology

Waterfall is a linear approach to a project. In this methodology, the sequence of events is something like:

1. Gather and document requirements

2. Design

3. Code and unit test

4. Perform system testing

5. Perform user acceptance testing (UAT)

6. Fix any issues

7. Deliver the finished product

In a true Waterfall project, each of these factors above represents a distinct stage, with each stage generally having to finish before the next one can begin. There is also typically a stage gate between each; for example, requirements must be reviewed and approved by the customer before design can begin.

There are good and bad things about the Waterfall approach. On the positive side:

- Agencies and clients agree on what will be delivered early in the life cycle. This makes planning and designing more straightforward.

- Progress is more easily measured, as the full scope of the work is known in advance.

- Throughout the stages it's possible for various members of the team to be involved, or to continue with other work, depending on the active phase of the project.

For example, a business analyst or strategist can learn about and document what needs to be done, while the creatives, marketers or developers are working on other projects.

A customer presence is not strictly required after the requirements phase.

Here are some issues we have seen when using a pure Waterfall approach:

- One area which almost always falls short is the effectiveness of requirements. Gathering and documenting requirements, in a way that is meaningful to a customer, is often the most difficult part. Customers are sometimes intimidated by details, and specific details, provided early in the project are required with this approach. In addition, customers are not always able to visualise the end result from a requirements document. Mockups and Wireframes can help, but there's no question that most end users have some difficulty putting these elements together with the kind of written requirements required for forming a good picture of what they will be getting.

- Another potential drawback of pure Waterfall development is the possibility that the customer will be dissatisfied with their delivered service. As all deliverables are based upon documented requirements, a customer may not see what will be delivered until it's almost finished. By this stage, changes can be difficult (and costly) to implement.

The Agile Methodology

Agile is an iterative, team-based approach to a project. This approach emphasises the rapid delivery of a service (or product) in complete functional components. Rather than creating tasks and schedules, all time is "time-boxed" into phases called "sprints." Each sprint has a defined duration (usually in weeks) with a running list of deliverables, planned at the start of the sprint.

Deliverables are prioritised by business value, as determined by the customer. If all planned work for the sprint cannot be completed, work is re-prioritised and the information is used for future sprint planning.

As work is completed, it can be reviewed and evaluated by the project team and customer, through daily builds and end-of-sprint demos. Agile relies on a very high level of customer involvement throughout the project, but especially during these reviews.

Some of the advantages of the Agile approach are easy to see:

- The customer has frequent and early opportunities to see the work being delivered, and to make decisions and changes throughout the project.

- The customer gains a strong sense of ownership by working extensively and directly with the project team throughout the project.

- If time to market is a greater concern than releasing a complete project, Agile can more swiftly produce a cut-down version of the project, which can be built upon in successive iterations.

- Service delivery is often more user-focused, usually because of more and frequent direction from the customer.

And, of course, there are some disadvantages:

- The very high degree of customer involvement, while great for the project, may present problems for some customers who simply may not have the time for, or interest in, this type of participation.

- Agile works best when members of the team are completely dedicated to the project.

- Because Agile focuses on time-boxed delivery and frequent re-prioritisation, it's possible that some items set for delivery will not be completed within the allotted time frame. Additional sprints (beyond those initially planned) may be needed, adding to the project cost. In addition, customer involvement often leads to additional work requested throughout the project. Again, this can add to the overall time and cost of the implementation.

- The close working relationships in an Agile project are easiest to manage when the team members are located in the same physical space, which is not always possible. However, there are a variety of ways to handle this issue, such as webcams, collaboration tools, etc.

It is important when considering hiring a Project Manager that they have experience in dealing with both Waterfall and Agile methodologies.

Waterfall projects tend to be more fixed price and Agile tend to me more time and materials based.

It requires a specific skill set to be able to deliver a fixed price project on time and on budget, as ordinarily if a PM has a background in Agile, or time and materials projects, they find it hard to shift to a fixed budget approach.

PSYCHOMETRICS

In this section, it's important to note that one of the most common mistakes we see in hiring PMs is the failure to understand that this role is a detailed one.

It's not always easy to stereotype the personas of the perfect roles, even with the help of psychometric testing, but it's important that we labour the point that most Account Managers do not have the level of focus on detail that a Project Manager will have.

We often see candidates who proclaim to be an AM / PM and yes, while that role is needed in the early days of Agency life, the sooner you recognise which of the two that person actually is, the better. Often we see extrovert personalities who interview well and who **on** the surface seem to have a good level of attention to detail.

Checking the above point at interview stage, should be given particular focus as attention to detail is an important character trait for a Project Manager. Could you devise a test for your potential Project Managers, to assess their true capability for the role? In the past, and this may come across as a broad generalisation, it is often the quieter, slightly more introverted characters who possess more of the traits required for success in the Project Manager role. They may not interview as well as their more extroverted counterparts, but they will in the long run prove more successful in the role.

WHAT'S IN IT FOR ME? (WIIFM)

Timesheeting is a subject that comes up frequently and has been a bit of a hot potato with some of the Agencies we have worked with in the past.

There is no question that some of the most efficient Agencies we have, worked with timesheets, and there are others for whom timesheeting just isn't their culture.

It's clear that timesheeting is an excellent way to solve delivery problems. If there is an issue, we can easily identify where clients are being over or under serviced. It can also help to identify areas where projects have been mis sold.

In our case, we used timesheeting to help make sure our team wasn't overstretched, and it was an excellent way to know where and when we needed to recruit next, and where we were light on sales.

Team members were told at Bluhalo, if you do nothing, record no time, you won't lose your job because of it. Have a job code called "I have nothing to do"! We constantly reminded our team they needed to deliver work promptly, and not fill dead times by over-servicing, unless that was specifically agreed.

That way, as we got busy, we became used to working at a certain pace, and could always fill the deadtime with internal projects if we needed to.

If your Agency has no delivery problems and makes money, then maybe you don't need to timesheet. To be honest, we never over-analysed the results, but the data was there should we need to look back over our shoulders and review what had gone wrong to improve the process moving forward.

The most efficient teams we've been involved with 100% use timesheets, and all of them tend to have one more Project Manager on average than they need, at every stage of their growth.

We would say that at least a dozen of these Agencies have some of the best cultures we've seen, so we don't always buy that timesheeting adversely affects culture. Yet we do accept that some Agency owners and teams are happier not to implement timesheeting in their Agencies.

Keep an open mind at different stages of growth; remember your Agency has different needs and that things change quickly!

It's vital that the whole team are aware of the studio timelines and resourcing. It helps sales and account management understand lead times, and where the gaps are. It's important to keep the studio running efficiently but at the same time to try NOT to become what we jokingly refer to as a sausage factory, where everything is so processed you lose every ounce of creativity.

This is where timesheets are needed, you can lose them later don't worry. Initially we need to understand exactly where you are at with each client.

It's important that you get the team fully bought in here. It's not about you, it's actually more about helping your team, they need to understand why you are doing this!

They need to know 'what's in it for me (or wiifm!)'. What are the team benefits to timesheeting?

- It ensures that clients are getting the correct information about time spent on their work.

- It helps you understand where you need to recruit next to help alleviate the pressure on people who are overstretched.

- It improves the business process so everyone can work smarter, not stupidly harder!

- It ensures that those who deliver the most value and billings are rewarded correctly.

It is important that timesheets of a minimum of eight hours are recorded daily. Allocate time to client, or internal projects or work, research, meetings; even being honest and saying I did nothing and I'm not feeling uncomfortable.

Regardless of whether you are using a timesheet tool, project management software or simple spreadsheets, you need to create a timesheet along these lines in order to understand who is billing what per month.

In the modern world of cloud accounting, and, for example, the ecosystem of add-on apps to Xero timesheeting, software can be easily integrated into your financial accounting system to aid better quality reporting of job profitability.

PROCESS WORKFLOW

The first step we took when creating our project delivery process was to map out the complete flow of every step in the life cycle of a project from winning the pitch to launching the project.

You could go one step further and start with marketing to attract leads through to your existing ongoing client service delivery experience.

Below is a screenshot of an example of how we started to write out the stages/steps to our process.

We then expanded into more of these sections listed below, with individual processes supporting each step.

Example:

Project Manager to expand project plan

Account Manager sends detailed project plan to client

Design

Client Feedback**

Design amends

Design sign off**

2ND Stage Payment

*Development mean either design and build or marketing planning (you may need to expand two routes here)

Development Kick off meeting (Producer, Creative, Develop)

Development Starts

Testing (Internal)

Producer and Creative QA

3RD Stage payment

Release for UAT**

Final Amends/ Snagging**

Clients Sign off for live**

Final Payment**

LIVE

Then ideally sold pre-project......

30 Day warranty** for bug fixes

Subject to contract – SLA/ Retainer / Handover**

VISUALISING PROCESS

After sorting out our project delivery process, the next stage was to visualise the process, in order for clients to be able to understand it more easily.

Initially we took a more formal approach, called the ISO9001 approach, where all our process workflows were documented and all our processes detailed in centralised folders for all to access. If you are not familiar with ISO9001, it is the international standard that specifies requirements for a quality management system within an organisation.

Overtime we tried to simplify this a little by adding external visuals in the studio. Ideally something publicly displayed for the whole team to see and not hidden away in a file structure somewhere.

We find that the Agencies who openly visualise process approaches on presentations – as well as when they are working in the studio – are often better at understanding the processes within the clients' businesses. They also help the wider team to respect and understand them.

We also would adapt cut down visual versions of the project delivery process to be inserted into our presentations to prospects and clients.

We learnt that over time the project management visuals really assisted us in presenting our delivery methodologies and approaches, helping us move from time to value selling. The earlier in the sale process we presented our delivery processes and methodologies, the easier it was to get the client to pay and buy into the value of our services.

Eventually everyone in our Agency knew the process inside out, and new starters could be inducted from day one into our delivery approach.

Of course, all good things break down over time, and we had to revisit parts of the process and improve our approach as we scaled, trying always to see these issues as challenges. We really recommend you fix one process issue at a time, rather than taking on too much in one go. Often one broken process that we identify and fix can resolve 80% of the delivery issues across all of our clients. So look out for the quick fixes that have the biggest impact and fix those broken processes first.

ALIGNMENT

Understanding capacity and billability helps you see whether the services you are selling are aligned with your current resource.

The success and failure of Agencies and their profitability often stems from the lack of alignment; of the services you sell with the resource you have available.

Once you have a full month's worth of timesheet data, do just two things:

Review how busy the team are:

- Where is their time going? Who is busy, who is quiet, why? Do you need to look at data over three months to get a better picture from the results?

Review client servicing:

- Are any clients under serviced? Or are some clients over serviced? Look at your processes to fix these issues as soon as possible.

The key thing initially is to make sure that your services are aligned to your billings and that the work in the studio is distributed fairly.

For example if you have a team of creatives, but you are only selling development or marketing, you have an alignment issue.

You will have to use freelancers, or recruit more people to help deliver these services. Of course, you could cross train your team to help cope with these alignment issues, but sometimes you need to accept that your client demand no longer matches your available skill set and if you cannot retrain your team, you will need to replace your team to be able to deliver the services you are offering.

The quicker you recognise that this is happening to you, and the quicker you act, the healthier your Agency will be.

GREAT EXPECTATIONS

Setting expectations with clients was one of the biggest lessons we learnt both in running our Agency and advising others.

Some Agencies go as far as making sure that during the pre-pitch stage, the clients have the necessary time and resource to manage the project and their commitments to it.

A useful example of the need to set expectations is when Agencies are developing any type of technology for a marketing client. It's almost standard for any new technology to have a period of testing, bug testing or integration testing, yet clients are often in shock at how long and how much work they need to do to assist in testing, or are horrified by how long the snag or bug lists are at the end of any development phase.

Telling customers up front to expect certain challenges at certain stages, means there are no surprises. Pitch it right and they may even celebrate that there are only 100 bugs or issues to fix, rather than suddenly demanding their money back or threatening legal action, which can happen all too regularly for these types of tech focused Agencies. Whatever type of Agency you are, we are sure you can relate to this example in one way or another.

Taking care not to over promise is another key part of expectation setting. We've worked with Agencies where the owners and new business teams are such incredibly enthusiastic salespeople that they always over promised and set unrealistic expectations of success. One particular team we know of never retained one client! They were setup to fail from the outset.

In these cases, the Agencies were so good at pitching that they set an unrealistic expectation of how fun or exciting the process was going to be.

The reality was that these clients had good delivery teams with solid people, but there was such a bump when coming down from the highs of the pitch process, to how the first discovery or planning session went, that it left the clients feeling like they may have chosen the wrong Agency. The delivery team could never match the expectations in service delivery set by the Agency sales team.

It's not about dampening down in pitching how the delivery process will go, but simply helping set the expectation at the outset really helps the team and clients success. It's more about making sure your pitch team contains a balanced team, a mix of people who are aiming to win the business, and as many of the people who are likely to work on moving forward that particular prospect's account so that there is an element of realism in what it will be like to work with your Agency.

Then, when onboarding the client, ensure that the client meets with as many of the team as possible. This will help you put together the delivery plan in a way that supersedes all the pitch promises that may arise in the future.

Remember the adage: Always under promise and over deliver.

UNDER PROMISE, OVER DELIVER

In our experience, most Agencies over service their clients -but there is a fine line between over servicing your clients an acceptable amount, or a moderate to excessive amount!

An acceptable amount would be up to 15%; a moderate to excessive amount would be over 15-20%; and an excessive amount would be over 20%. If you lose one client that is less than 15% of your income, then in most cases, this will be less than or equal to the Agency's annual profits This would mean, for a short period of time the Agency would be at a break even point and with that, focus can bounce back quickly.

Any client losses over 15% could mean having to lose staff in the short term.

The first thing you need to understand, is over servicing an issue, then where exactly is the over servicing coming from.

1. Was it because you mis-sold the work in the first place? Either you misunderstood what was required or you simply didn't budget enough time to complete the task in relation to the client's expectation.

2. Your sales team agreed a price that just wasn't realistic. Was it that? Even though you quoted correctly and realistically, poor initial planning meant the project was approached in the wrong way from the outset?

3. Was it because the team were poorly project managed, or not capable enough to deliver the project efficiently?

It may well turn out to be a combination of some or all of the above.

The most important thing about over servicing is that you are able to identify when it starts happening as soon as possible. Once you've recognised it's there, seek to improve the sales, project kick off or project delivery process one step at a time. By taking one project and fixing the process around it, you will usually fix all the issues and future problems you have around over servicing.

Of course learning lessons on over servicing can be costly and can cause clients to be distressed or unhappy, as inevitably delays in the project delivery can occur.

Additionally, the Agency can start to resent the client, because of all of the extra time you've invested in their project, potentially with little or no appreciation.

Over the years we have learnt that it's the pre-delivery planning stage that's the key to nailing the expectations.

As the old adage goes;

A woodsman was once asked, "What would you do if you had just five minutes to chop down a tree?" He answered, "I would spend the first two and a half minutes sharpening my axe."

Let us take a few minutes to sharpen our perspective.

DAY RATES

Having the wrong (on the low side) day rate will affect profitability. No matter how well you sell, project manage or deliver your services, without the correct day rate you will be fighting a losing battle.

We touched on setting your day rates a little earlier in the Finance section of this book, mainly getting you to focus on a competitive market rate - however we can now expand on this in more detail.

There are typically three ways to approach day rates. The first way is as follows:

Add up your total (overhead). Let's say it's £700,000 (Overhead).

Then work out the number of days you have available to sell through your team (Capacity). Let's say you have 1400 days available to sell:

Then it's (Overhead) (£) /Capacity (days)

Break Event Day Rate

£700,000 / 1400 = £500 a day to break even.

With most Agencies making between 10-30% operating profit, adding £150 (30%) to make the day rate £650, would give you both a margin and some protection against you not filling your capacity.

The second option, the one we talked about in the Finance section, would be to carry out some market research to understand what the market day rates are for your services and then set a price you feel comfortable with based on that.

For example your breakeven day rate is £500 per day and the market rate is £880. You then charge £880 knowing that you are not only competitive on price and have the ability to make a healthier profit margin, but also know you have extra protection to absorb some of the over servicing you give to your clients.

The third option is used when you are confident of the extra value you bring. In this case, you may be able to focus more on the outcomes, the results or the value (direct and indirect) that the work you are doing will bring.

For example, let's say your competitors charge £880 a day, and you charge £1,280, because you know that your results are typically far better than your competitors. So the client paying a little more per day, may generate tens of thousands of increased revenues, or a greater return on investment through your approach or the quality of your team. We call this value selling.

WORKING STYLES

Even with the best project management, processes, and correct day rates, without motivated quality team members who understand the importance of the work they are doing, you may still not be able to deliver work effectively.

Your Project Managers will understand which team members work in which way, the ones who are faster or slower to deliver. The team members who maybe make the most mistakes and the ones who need the least support.

For all of these reasons, it's often useful to get Project Managers involved in a small way with the recruitment process, as a means of trying to establish potential team member's working and delivery styles.

Chapter 6: Agency Tribal Structures

4-4-2 or 5-3-2?

So if I may, I (Spencer) would like to continue to share the story of my Agency journey to £1m in revenue.

When you start out, you are a one-man band. You work in stages; you sell, then you deliver, or you sell and bring in other people (freelancers) to deliver.

The advantage of this is that your overheads are low, and, if you are smart, you will have an integrated work life/balance. You may, however, risk not moving with the times without others around you.

Occasionally, partnerships of three or four people start a business together. In this case, it is crucial that everyone understands their role or roles in the company to ensure sharp decision-making and no crossed wires.

The more focused everyone is, and the less procrastination or over-collaboration on decisions, the more success you will have, and your business will progress more effectively.

Recruiting your first employee

Whoever you are, the time will come when you need to hire team members. It is a familiar source of confusion, however, with business owners often asking: "Who? What? Where? When?".

In year one of my (Spencer) business, K2 Consulting (before it became Bluhalo), my turnover was £30,000. This was a much lower year one sales and wages number than when I was employed by an Agency. Although a difficult position to be in, I had the freedom to work for myself, even if I was paid less!

Midway through year two, I was earning more than I had previously, taking in the sum of £60,000 (and projecting a £90k-120k year) a year, but at a price.

I was constantly working. I sold all day and designed and coded all night. My lifestyle business was giving me no life!

If I wasn't selling, I was in delivery mode and vice versa, so my sales were inconsistent. This also meant that though I was constantly busy, I was stuck in an eternal feast or famine loop.

At this stage, I decided to take someone on. I wanted to step up to take in £12,000 a month as opposed to £6,000. The problem was, where would this new person fit into the company? Would I sell and they design and code? Or would I design and code and get someone in to sell?

The path I took, and the one I would usually recommend is best, was to make myself, the owner, the Sales/Account/Project Manager and then to bring someone in to deliver the services I sold.

There is always someone out there who is great at delivery, but no one will work harder to sell your company to clients than you. In service businesses, people must trust who they buy from, and no one more genuinely represents a business more than its owner, especially in early stages of the company.

I took on a developer and assumed my new role as new Business/Account/Project Manager. It was hard to entrust such a huge chunk of my business to someone else and, in the short term, give away such a large sum of my salary before seeing a return.

But I was looking forward to sharing the workload and cutting back on the hours and all-nighters, well at least for a bit!

As a two-man band, ideally, you'll have a straightforward structure. One of you sells and manages a client, one delivers. Simple. Once these two positions are separated, the quicker and better business will come.

One year on from recruiting my first developer and now in my second year of trading, my sales were consistent, and my turnover had doubled, so I could pay myself more. Although the long hours didn't subside, they weren't as bad.

Business life is often a case of two steps forward, one step back. But just be assured you are still getting somewhere. A step back in earnings may get you closer to a scalable business, as you have more free cash to invest in infrastructure and also the chance to increase your future earnings, or at that point to choose a more balanced lifestyle.

One fundamental problem for some business founders is the separation. Don't become too fixated on the delivery of your business because you will start making excuses not to sell. If this is the case, the hire must be the other way around. We will talk more about the sales role later on in this book.

Now what?

The rule from here on is to try and create somewhere between £6k to £8k a month in revenues of a particular service for each person you recruit. Remembering that once on board each billable staff member should be billing between £8k to £12k (£10k on average) per month.

However, at all stages in Agency growth, you will have the opportunity to pitch for a step-change deal. That is, a deal that will take you up to the next level.

This new business win can help you develop rapidly. For instance, I won a deal that enabled me to go from two to eight people overnight.

These sorts of deals not only help you grow, but often open you up to a world of new business opportunities and connections in new sectors.

I had the opportunity to pitch to build an ecommerce site for a well-known high street jeweller. The deal was £30,000 for three months' work. In the meantime, I found an existing team of six people who had the skills to build such a site but whose business was struggling.

I knew then that if I won the deal, I could recruit them into Bluhalo and we could work on the project and I could then offer more technical services.

That is precisely what happened. I won the contract and took on the extra people from the struggling tech start up. I now found myself with a team of eight.

It was a risky move; I was still only turning over £10,000 a month at that stage, and this new deal would take me £20,000 per month for three months. However, I had eight people on my team, and if we stick to our rule, the numbers wouldn't stack up. With eight people at £6k per person, I should have been at £48,000 per month not £20,000 to make this work.

The extra sales did not come quickly, suddenly the numbers were not working, major lesson here, I had to downsize my team of eight to six immediately.

A team of six people at £6k billing per head are £36k. We were now doing £18-20k in monthly revenues and my calculated risk was failing.

I was not paying myself. I want to add we had low wage cost and no office rent, so there were other factors involved in how we managed to survive.

At this stage let me show you my staff numbers I used to scale from £0-£3m.

Turnover (rounded)	Team Size	Billings Per Head
£30,000	1	£30k
£90,000	2	£45k
£169,000	6	£28k
£250,000	8	£31k
£512,000	10	£51k
£1,400,000	25	£56k
£2,000,000	30	£66k
£2,500,000	40	£63k
£3,000,000	32	£94k

As you can see, at this point, I was nowhere near my recommended benchmark and the numbers Pete and I work to today with clients.

So, like me, you may have to accept that in the early years you will probably sweat your cash flow to scale, and sometimes there will be some calculated risks to take.

Eventually, my Non-Exec gave me sales targets and those took me from £20k per month to £42k per month within six months which at the time, turned the business around. The year after we hit our first £1m in sales.

There are six pieces of advice for Agencies who want to smash through the £1m barrier:

1. Have a clear vision of getting to £1m.

2. Have clear targets that you have to keep hitting.

3. Think and act as a bigger Agency than you are now.

4. Deliver great work.

5. Separate client services from project management.

6. Build your Agency marketing momentum.

Post £1m

Most Agencies, when they start, embrace the "This is my business, I'll run it my way, friendly, family, lifestyle approach". This family approach typically lasts up to the first £1m-£1.5m.

At that point, the business can afford to recruit more "grown-ups", a term to describe people who can bring more experience and value to the organisations and start to put in some structure to help it grow to the £2-£3m level and beyond.

Most Agencies we have encountered, who despite having a good spread of clients, struggle to scale beyond the £1.2m to £1.5m mark. They often think they are struggling because of a delivery, sales or cash flow reason, but have in fact got the wrong organisational structure in place, which causes the root problem.

We often encounter at this stage, too high a headcount (so not enough cash) or too low a headcount (so not enough resource) in the Agency for the turnover to grow.

Moving from £1m to £1.5m was one of our most significant hurdles and is still one of the most common tasks we undertake in helping Agencies today.

We call breaking the £1.5m turnover barrier, "breaking the hump," as we affectionately call it, and for most Agencies it is a difficult time. Some Agencies do manage to push through this level as we did at Bluhalo, but at the £2.2m turnover mark we had around 40 staff.

As I explained earlier, at £3m with 34 staff, we were structured more effectively, and still delivered great work. We were selling value, not time. Team morale was great and we had happy clients - it all just worked.

The key at this point was getting the team structures right as they are paramount to scaling.

There are three approaches to this stage.

It's a personal choice:

1. Traditional Pyramid type structure.

2. Horizontal Flat/ Vertical type structures.

3. A hybrid of the two.

PYRAMID & PODS

We always say "if your structure works for you and your team, and the business doesn't have problems it can't fix, then leave it!" If it already works then don't try and fix it.

Having a talented group of people who are happy at work, and with the way their team is structured, is as powerful as you embracing someone else's system or approach to organisational structure.

A good organisational structure needs a team behind it who believe and buy into it!

This section is designed for troubleshooting: to help those of you who have issues in your structure, processes that can't seem to be fixed, an unhappy team, or as a business you are struggling to break through certain levels.

A useful example is when we received a call to help an Agency with its sales process.

They were convinced they had a sales process issue. We quickly identified that it was in fact an organisational structure issue.

No sales process could fix the problem with people working in the wrong roles in the Agency. We call this, people sitting in the wrong seats.

The team was structured in a way that meant the sales team could never get the information it needed to process quotes, proposals and pitches effectively.

What do we mean by a Pyramid and Pod organisational structure in an Agency?

We see two typical types of structure in an Agency.

1. A Pyramid or Hierarchical structure

A pyramid organisation is a traditional layout, a structure that is vertical, where the organisation starts with a CEO with typically five reports, covering each part of the business; the reports also have reports, and a hierarchical type structure is formed.

Jim Collin's book "Good to Great" and Gino Wickman's book "Get a Grip/Traction" are both excellent reads for people looking to build these kinds of structures.

Before you do implement this structure (if you haven't already) or you are looking to change, we really recommend you read Frederic Laloux's book "Reinventing Organizations", which covers the history and the future of the way companies are structured.

2. A Pod or Flat structure.

A flat or pod structure usually involves little or no hierarchy. The approach being that people are grown-ups; they don't need power or people to manage them. They have roles and responsibilities and are empowered, trusted to be autonomous in their role. They are built often with a meritocratic approach, where people are rewarded on merit not position.

Pod structures are flat organisational structures, but they have client focussed teams at the heart of their service. We find Agencies can really suit these types of teams.

This structure is usually made up of the following team members:

- One client facing team member such as an Account Manager/Director

- One delivery focused person, a Project Manager

- One person who is focused on defining the strategy, discovery and or the scope of works to be carried out.

- This role is often called a Producer, Planner, Strategist, Business Analyst, but is tailored to the Agency service delivery type.

As pods get larger they can add a fourth person to split out strategy/planning.

In our Agency, we called the Pod's Eco-Team's. They were self-sufficient business units within the Agency. Typically, they managed around £650k to £1m per unit in fees.

Brian J Robertson's Holacracy is another approach to flat structures. While we haven't seen an Agency embrace this approach yet, there are many cut down versions of this format, which lends itself to the Agency Model.

Choosing between Pyramids and Pods.

Normally, you will have an opinion one way or another. Reading more on this comprehensive subject will help you decide what better suits your people and culture.

Having worked with many Agencies, the structures are often driven by the owner, leadership team and their personal values and culture. Consider getting help from outside the business to help implement a change in the organisational structure. The investment in knowledge and experience in this area will help increase the likelihood of a successful outcome.

ABR Principle

Agencies are sales led.

You are "always be interviewing", but "only be actually offering" once the sales are ready.

When you win a project, you can then recruit new people. As we've said earlier in the book, you should almost never recruit people then find clients. It's just too risky. Unless you have extreme confidence or the cash to allow you to take some risks.

We repeat this over and over in this book because it's too important not to! Your wage cost is your largest overhead. You need to keep this carefully aligned to make profit.

The problem is, the hiring process can take Agencies anything from an eight week period to around four months. Usually, once you have won new business above and beyond your current capacity, you have only about four weeks (maximum) to find someone new - so that they can start working on the new project.

So what you should be doing is recruiting constantly. Interview three-four people a week and develop a talent pool for when you need to hire quickly. Make it clear to potential employees that you are always looking for new talent.

Then when you do win a new deal, and the contracts are being signed, you are perfectly poised to appoint the people you have been lining up to work for you.

Do be realistic; if you win a huge new client you won't be able to employ all those fantastically talented new people at short notice. And bear in mind, that once you recruit these people, you need to be out there finding them ongoing work, well before the project is finished. If you cannot do this, then you'll have to make redundancies.

When you have a spike in sales, it will make sense to recruit freelancers - but be cautious for the reasons outlined later in this chapter.

When you are growing your Agency from £5m upwards, you may find you need to keep a certain percentage of your workforce flexible to help with the alignment issue we talked about in Chapter five.

It's worth noting that if you do choose to bring in freelancers as an alternative to recruiting full time headcount, it probably goes without saying that your profit levels will be hit quite hard; we see this in nine out of ten cases. It hurt us, which is why when we were at £3.5m turnover, Bluhalo's freelance budget was only £2k per month, (mainly for pitch support) and we made that work though it wasn't always easy, we did prove it was possible. Selling only what you can deliver, and aligning sales and resource carefully.

PEOPLE ARE YOUR ONLY ASSET

When Bluhalo started as K2; as a one-man band Agency owner, Spencer went to visit his friend's Agency. She had a team of 10 staff in her impressive mews office in London. Four were permanent members of the team, and the remaining six were brought in as freelancers to help deliver current projects and other projects, when and where she needed them to help.

Eight years down the line, Bluhalo had 50 members of staff while my friend still had four members of permanent staff, and a handful of freelancers on standby.

Every time we won business we recruited and pressured ourselves into winning more. We made sure we hit our sales' targets so we could afford to pay our ever-growing wage bill.

However Spencer's friend didn't have this pressure. Since she only used freelancers, there was never any pressure to keep hitting the sales' targets. If she missed a target, she just didn't use the freelancers.

Maybe she had got it right in one way - we think in the short term her life would have been less stressful than ours. It can be tough managing employees and aligning them to the revenue spikes that happen in those early years. Though in financial terms, 10 years later she had to shut down her Agency, while we sold ours for millions.

We remember at the time thinking that if you commit to your business it will commit back. Yes it's a commitment to recruit, but one that will force you to move the business forward.

The other challenge with freelancers is that there's often no sense of accountability or ownership from them.

They get to walk out when their time is up, and the rest of the team can sometimes get left to pick up the pieces. It's also not great for morale when you are earning in a week what someone sitting next to you is earning in a day.

Of course we feel there are some occasions where freelancers are invaluable - such as when extra pitch support is needed or when unique one-off pieces of work are required. Freelancers could also be useful to help deliver a niche project, or adding valuable expertise to your existing team's knowledge. Just make sure that you don't get caught up in the cycle of having permanent freelancers unless you really can justify doing so.

Our expertise and experience tell us that if you have up to £4-5m (50-60 staff) you should not need to use freelancers, other than on rare occasions, to deliver any tactical work your team can't do; or to deal with spikes in revenue that will be short lived like a client using you on a short contact.

With our budget for freelancers a mere £2k a month at £3.5m in revenue, we sold around our team and their capacity and partnered with other Agencies for work we did not do. We did not have the need to have pools of contractors around ready to support us with their day rate equivalents of £75-£125k salaries.

We were committed to finding billings for our team, despite the fast-changing landscape.

The reality is though once you are above 50 full-time employees, you may be forced to use the flexibility of freelancers to help you scale up and down.

Remember in an Agency, people are your only real asset.

Our consultancy, Cactus, is a collaborative economy business, we have no offices, no structure, are based in different countries and some of our people belong to the gig economy (are self-employed). Agencies and service businesses are starting to adopt these types of models.

This means that they are effectively Agencies full of team members who are not full-time employees.

This is an exciting and interesting development for future Agency models. With the ever increasing demand from Agency employees for more flexible working, we suspect that gig economy people in this mode will take more ownership of the work they do on a project, rather than work on a time basis - but let's see how Agency future model pans out! Certainly worth looking at Agencies like www.upthereeverywhere.com as a good example. We'll talk more about some of these changes later in the chapter

UNRAVELLING SPAGHETTI

The number one challenge for small Agencies trying to grow is to create the ideal team structure. A team of people with specialist skills doing specific roles, not a team of people with specific or wider skills doing lots of different roles. It's an important shift for Agencies to make, we often label this situation that Agencies are in as 'Spaghetti', where people in the business end up working not just one role but several. This is common for Agencies in their early trading years. The key is to move the Agency from a team of generalists to a team of specialists.

For example, early stage Agencies tend to develop lots of hybrid roles such as an Account/Project Manager or a Developer who liaises with customers. The owner and others can have so many roles that it's hard to perform one effectively.

We spend a lot of our time unravelling the spaghetti to help team members own specialist roles and responsibilities.

We still walk into Agency teams of over 30 people and discover the Agency owner is CEO/MD, Account Manager, sometimes programming and also heavily involved with all stages of recruitment.

At 30 full time employees, as the owner, you should be in the position where you are only focusing on your Agency's vision, leadership and culture.

We understand that at times in the business, finances can dictate what you can and cannot do.

Of course recruiting for specialist roles in the early stages is not always financially possible. However, the minute you have enough revenue to support the extra salaries, you should create more specific and specialised roles.

Do not fall into the trap of employing two people who are both Account and Project Managers. Have one of each, and the reward will be much higher. That way everyone understands their own position, there are no crossed wires, and your staff can get on with what they are good at.

Making sure your project staff: Designers, Developers, Marketers, etc, bill their time for the planning and creation of work and Account Managers do the client communication means that the actual work is completed more efficiently.

The added benefit of having focused Account and Project Managers is that the client knows who they should be addressing their ideas or grievances to, and this minimises discussion time. Having the team stick to their assigned roles, frees them from repetition, hesitation or deviation, and your people will inevitably have more time to benefit your business.

Of course, the needs of businesses change over time, and once you have grown sufficiently to employ enough specialists, then you may want to consider adding generalists to your team.

There are exceptions to the advice we have just provided you with. Sometimes, when your business is more established, it can be beneficial to have generalists because of the flexibility they can bring.

As you scale, it can get trickier to align sales with resource, we discussed the importance of "alignment" earlier in the book, so cross skilling and creating some non-specific roles can add a level of flexibility that will really help.

And sometimes, a more experienced generalist can provide backup to different parts of the team, as and when you should need it.

THE HOLY GRAIL

We often get asked what metrics we use for scaling an Agency: Here is our guide taking into account both industry benchmarks and our experience.

Minimum annual billing per employee

Try this simple sum. Take the fee billings (excluding paid media and pass through costs) for the last three months and times by four, to get an annualised figure. Then divide this by the total number of staff you have. The absolute minimum here should be £60-£65k.

For example:

If your fee only billings for the last quarter are £300k – multiplied by four, gives an annualised run rate of £1.2m. If you have 17 staff at this point you are circa £70k per employee. This is at an acceptable level.

Larger Agencies of £4m of fee income and over should see this increase to £90-£100k of billings per annum.

As you get economies of scale and grow the Agency, these numbers will increase to typically £75k per annum per person (£1-2m), and then £85k per annum per person (£2m), then ideally £85-£100k* per annum per person (£3m+).

*£100k revenue per person per annum is recognised as the holy grail for Agencies.

Wages/Gross Profit Ratio

In addition, due to salary fluctuations by region, skill set or client size, you will also need to keep an eye on your wage cost to gross profit ratio.

Larger Agencies will work to 55%. We say a normal business should be 58-63% and a growing business around 63-68%.

At <55% your team may well be under pressure, working very hard. At > 70% you will be either recruiting ahead of an impending sales curve, or more likely need to be cutting overhead.

Salary to Billings Ratio – a rough rule of thumb

We like to see each individual fee earner billing around 3x their salary as a rough guide. Please note this can vary slightly, but usually a member of the billable team, who is billing themselves regularly out at circa £120k per annum (10k per month average), is probably worth a £40k salary. As a further example, an employee billing £180k in billings per annum, would in this example, be worth paying a £60k salary.

Other points to consider

It's important to recognise the indirect and often hidden value some people bring to the business as well as the direct billings.

For example, a Project Manager may not bill three times their salary, in fact it may be more like one to two times, however, through their ability to run projects efficiently, they may save the Agency thousands or hundreds of thousands of pounds a year in efficiency, indirectly helping billable resource to push out more.

As you scale to the first £1m, you are effectively moving from people wearing too many hats to people wearing just one.

In other words you are moving them from general roles and responsibilities to more specific ones.

Some Agencies who freelance out through these early stages, or those with one larger client, can run more profitably and generate more free cash. Those Agencies often suffer with the shift later to recruiting or breaking the one large client dominance.

In these situations, it's important to be pragmatic and work out between you and your business partners which roles you will each undertake.

Where possible, make sure one of you is managing and focusing on the external part of the business and one of you managing and focusing on the internal part of the business. That way you have at least one of you externally focussed on sales/marketing, and at least one of you internally focused on the operational and delivery part of the Agency.

As you continue along the journey, there will be other important investments in roles you will need to recruit in order to help the business grow further. We are often asked about when to hire these roles as you approach £1m and move on towards the £2m level.

Of course, there are many factors to making these decisions, if finance and cash flow or reserves allow, then yes, recruit a Marketing Manager as early as possible to help drive leads, then a sales person.

There is always an element of calculated risk with taking on these roles.

We typically see these roles coming in at the following points, should cash flow allow:

- Marketing Manager £70 -£80k per month.

- Talent Manager £130-170k per month (or typically 7-10 recruits in the year ahead including predicted churn).

- Business Development Manager £80k-120k per month window, about six months after the Marketing Manager starts.

- Administration Office Manager/Finance (PT) at £50k per month and then separated as two roles by £70-£100k per month.

Again, if cash allows, the sooner you bring on the above roles, the better the business will scale.

There are of course two ways to scale:

- Find business and recruit behind the curve.

- Hire ahead of the sales growth curve.

For us, the former is always the safest and we've mentioned this a lot in this book. There will be exceptional times however when the latter is the smart play.

As an Agency, your wage cost is your most significant overhead, and therefore you must embrace the ABR (Always Be Recruiting) strategy we spoke about in chapter five.

Make sure you are appointing candidates in line with the new business wins. It doesn't make sense just to have people sitting around waiting for the business to grow, there is a fine line between profit and growth, and people more than often are the cost that separates the two.

When you find yourself with cash in the bank, beyond what you need, you may be able to make tactical recruits ahead of the curve. A few of those hires may well help you scale, such as the Marketing Manager role, but do manage these situations carefully.

Organisational structures are often very hard in these early stages; there is no question that once you have passed £1.5m fee income mark, with the right structure, whether pyramid (vertical) or pods/flat, the business becomes more stable, and by 30 people, or £2m plus in fee income, you finally should be in a position to work *on* the business, not *in* the business.

From £1m to £5m

As we scaled Bluhalo we introduced eco-teams, or pods as we now call them, self-sufficient client managing teams.

We think this approach has been one of the most empowering for the Agency owners we've worked with, as it helps transfer ownership of client management and delivery into a team of three, allowing the owners to focus on the business holistically, without being dragged into the day to day running of the Agency.

This is a vast subject to cover in a way which will satisfy everyone's level, so let us start with some Agencynomics for you.

As we wrote earlier, when building an Agency, the Utopia is to achieve £100k turnover per person per annum (that's provided you have a gross profit figure of more than 85%). If it's less, you need to increase proportionally. This will help you explain those annoying league tables where you see each employee billing £250k per person per annum. What you don't realise is that those Agencies typically have a high Cost of Sale, so the number is artificially high.

So, at £100k per person per annum that's a £1m turnover with 10 full time employees.

Well, of course, we did say this was Utopia!

It would indeed be hard for most Agencies to achieve this level of turnover per head for a good few years.

We would say an Agency of £3m in revenues and above should be getting closer to this number; we reached £94k at £3M for example in 2008. We want to make it clear there are positive factors why you may not hit this number. Investing ahead of a sales curve to grow faster is one.

A NEW WORLD ORDER

Business transformation is firmly fixed on the Agency landscape.

There has been a real shift in focus from profit to purpose, hierarchies to flat structures, from organisations that are more directive and controlling to ones where autonomous empowered work forces are in place.

There is an increased demand for organisational openness and transparency.

The nature of Agencies certainly aligns itself with these more modern, less traditional approaches to Agency organisational structures and practices.

Peter Drucker referred to the Knowledge Organisation and Frederick Laloux to Green and Teal organisations. These, and other readings on the subject, are detailed in the back of this book.

Aside from all the huge benefits Agency employees often receive, from 2017 we have already seen a shift in Agencies starting to trial or even fully convert to alternative models. From appointing their employees to become shareholding partners, removing all management roles, introduce self-selected pay structures, reducing the typical five day 40 hour week to a four day 30 hour working week and unlimited paid vacation.

We frequently speak on the future Agency model; as we spoke about earlier in the book, we already see the impact of the Collaborative Economy Agencies creating new models, with no offices, gig economy staff and no office or full-time staff.

The changing business economy in the following areas is having an impact on all businesses including Agencies.

All of these models are already, or soon could be, impacting on the future of Agency models.

- Circular Economy

- Gig Economy

- Sharing Economy

- Peer Economy

- On-demand Economy

- Access Economy

- Collaborative Consumption

There are already some exciting new models including: pop-up Agencies, Agencies who only work remotely in their clients offices, Agencies who are co-owned by the clients: It's very important to firmly keep one eye on the new emerging Agency business models, as well as the demands and needs of both your clients and prospective clients, to make sure they are aligned.

Chapter 7: Agency Anthropology

HAPPY TEAM, HAPPY CLIENT

Although we've heard it a million times, Peter Drucker's famous quote "Culture eats strategy for breakfast", is very true.

From our personal experience, there is no question that a culture with the right collective mindset will outperform any Agency with a great strategy yet lacking in the right mindset.

Let's not also forget the old adage "Happy team, happy client". Client expertise cannot truly exist in our opinion unless there is a great culture within the Agency.

We also talked earlier about values when working on Agency positioning.

While core values are important, so is cultural contribution.

It's very wise to understand these three areas when building your Agency culture.

1. Permission to play values

These are the standards that every organisation should think of as essential (values such as honesty, integrity, respect for others).

2. Accidental values

Accidental values arise spontaneously. They usually reflect the common interests or personalities of the organisation's employees. Accidental values can be good for a company, such as when they create an atmosphere of inclusivity.

3. Aspirational values

Often, core values in the early days of an Agency reflect the values of the company's founders.

Aspirational values are those that you'd like your Agency to accomplish in the future, but currently lack.

There are three key things that generate a positive work environment and that attract and keep good people in your business. These are listed below:

Aligned vision

You need to let employees know where the Agency is going, and where they fit into that journey personally. No one wants to work in an insecure environment so let people know if you intend to grow. Tell them what brands you hope to work with. Let them know of the career opportunities that will arise on the Agency's journey and show them how they can earn a higher salary as part of this plan.

Take the time to talk to individuals and understand what they would like from both their job and their life outside of work, and review this as often as possible.

If you align your organisation with the goals of individuals, then your people will become invested in your organisation. For a small Agency this may take the form of informal one to one meetings, and for larger businesses, this may be via more formal appraisals. Either way, it is important to get this done.

Don't be afraid to understand an employee's three, five, 10 year plan and life goals; align them to yours and even if the plan is to split away at some point from each other's journey, be open and help them on their journey to join the dots in their life moving forward.

People throw around the importance of "purpose" these days, but it's important that purpose applies to not only your employee's personal life goals, but also that their purpose aligns with their professional goals too. When an organisation and an employee can align both, that's when the magic happens in an organisation.

Continuous learning

It's essential to make sure your employees learn something new every day. Invest in training and keep their brains stimulated. If your staff are bored, it is inevitable that they would want to leave at some point in the near future. We often see training budgets unused, make it your responsibility to inspire the people in your team to continually invest towards mastery of their abilities.

Feeling valued and engaged as a valuable part of your Agency community.

Ensure you are paying a fair rate to each of your team relative to the roles they play. Most people are reasonable about what they feel they should be paid, and just want to be paid what they are worth. Wages are not an area to try and skimp on, because ultimately if your team are happy, they will work harder and make you more money.

It's important to reward the people who work hard, and show them how valuable they are and how they can add more value to the company and to themselves; they will appreciate this and ultimately, they will contribute more to the Agencies success.

WORK, REST AND DUVET DAYS

The only asset in an Agency is its people. Talent is at the heart of all Agencies. As we've explained before, they are your biggest overhead and, while there is always a level of healthy staff turnover, your clients want to have a consistent 'people experience' with their Agency of choice.

It is therefore very important that your Agency has a solid attraction and retention strategy to employ and retain top talent.

Do some research and be innovative at finding ways of recruiting the best in the business and the rising stars. Continuously think of reasons why people would want to work for you. Be bold. Be different.

Consider other benefits such as remote or flexible working where and when possible. Ensure that the working environment is the best it can be and consider what could make you different from, and more attractive to work with than other Agencies. Be creative; it needn't cost you a fortune. Duvet days, away days, late starts following company nights out are all ingenious ways of getting people to know you care about them.

Take time to review your team personas too; it may be that no-one owns a house in your company but it's their number one aspiration. How could you help solve that for example? Perhaps you could offer a save as you earn scheme to help people towards a deposit for their first home?

Here are some of our favourite ideas for attracting and retaining staff:

- Employee personal support services.

- Sending partners birthday cards/gifts.

- 25 days leave, birthday holiday and one extra day for every year they work for you up to 30 capped.

- £50pm budget per person for personal development.

- Flexible working.

- Time to work on "in the community projects".

- £50 per person per year to spruce up their desk.

- Pet Insurance.

- In-house massage.

- Office pamper days.

- In-house nutritionist.

- Free flu jabs.

- Social committee to organise team events.

- Cycle to work scheme.

- Lunchtime gym classes.

- Regular free breakfasts or lunches.

- Snacks and fresh fruit in the office.

- Free Netflix/Spotify/Amazon Prime subscriptions

Take a look at The Sunday Times 100 Best Companies to work for list and read up on the company profiles. See what they offer their staff as inspiration for your own offering.

Sense check all the benefits you want to offer to your team with your friendly accountant, who can advise you the best way to structure these benefits in order that you minimise tax liabilities where possible.

Try to ensure that the company indirectly picks up any taxable benefits costs rather than the employee.

CORNERSTONES

As you grow your Agency, there will be a few people who were there from the beginning or early stages, and hopefully you are planning to take them on the journey with you.

From one to 10 team size, it's quite likely that you won't lose many of your team. You'll be very proud of your low staff turnover. This is typically a sign that you are recruiting well and in line with your core values, either deliberately, or based on your gut feel of who is a culture fit or not.

Also, your Agency location will help those of you who are outside of the main cities. Agencies in a major city can find that their staff turnover can be higher naturally as there is just more opportunity to move and progress more frequently.

As you scale over time people will move on, but some people will be loyal for many years. Some can't leave as they are your fellow Directors, some people will be there for you through the ups and downs of business life. Perhaps they will stay under the promise that as you grow, they will grow with you; first in, the higher up the value chain they will become.

The important thing is to invest in those people so that they can grow personally and continue to add value. Otherwise one day the business will outgrow them and as the Agency changes, their role may get superseded.

We only retained five people from the original team of 15 people that we had around the £750k turnover mark through to the point at which we sold the business. One left to set up a joint business. The other two we invested in continually and their roles developed several times over the years into more senior positions; both of their salaries doubled over that period. One of our proudest moments now is to look at an old organisation chart and see that in fact 80% of the team now run their own Agencies or have very senior positions in large companies.

If you have multiple Directors, it is imperative that each of you honestly review your personal future and your future role within the organisation.

It's crucial that you are honest about your future at the company. If your ambition lies elsewhere, give your partners the opportunity to help you leave and let them continue the journey amicably.

Too many times we see one Director wanting something different to the other two or three, and all three go around in circles never managing to agree on a mutually beneficial plan.

We've had some Directors leave and take that "Distracting should be a separate business" with them to great success. We've seen Directors being bought out amicably and others who've bought out in a more distressing process.

The most important thing is that you are honest with each other about your journeys and align them. Keep reinvesting in yourselves and your team and be clear about your mutual ambitions.

TALENT SCOUT

We covered this earlier as one of the important non-billable/investment roles in an Agency. Part-time or depending on the size of the Agency, full-time talent management is essential in an Agency business. There are a couple of approaches to this.

Firstly, hire or retain someone who can help you find and keep the best talent. Someone who focuses more on the attraction and retention, rather than HR management, and train up someone operationally in the legal and process side of HR, like your Finance or Office Manager or hand this over to a third-party company.

At first this may seem like a cost prohibitive role, but if you look at your hiring plan for the next year and it has more than five people in it, with the possibility of one or two people from the existing team leaving, then you can see how this would pay itself in not having to pay the recruitment Agency fees on each hire.

The time saved by you and the team on continually resourcing candidates, managing initial interviews, checking core values and culture, as well as organising tests and personality profiling, will also significantly free up the Director's time, which can be better spent elsewhere.

To put things in perspective, when you consider multiple candidates and multiple stage interviews, finding seven roles could take as many as 50 interviews.

WOOD FROM THE TREES

Support and advice for your business typically comes in four forms:

1. Mentors (free).
2. Business Advisors (paid).
3. Specialist Non-Execs (paid).
4. Professional and Personal Coaches (paid).

While there is no doubt that there is a crossover between these four positions, our experience defines each role as follows:

The Mentor

This is usually someone who you highly respect, possibly someone who has achieved much success in their career, and has vast experience of many business types.

Many mentors are not paid for, though it is polite and sensible to lunch or wine and dine them. In return they will share their experience and wisdom, and you gain valuable advice for free.

In a very few cases mentors have been known to help out in return for a small percentage of equity in the Agency, but this is uncommon. If they are to be compensated in some way, it would be better to engage with them or someone else on a more formal basis.

The Business advisor

You could use a Management Consultant who has been formally trained and has experience of a variety of business models.

These people tend to have general skills and a technical approach to business. Typically, their experience is of being part of a business management team.

You could choose a Business Advisor who has experience of running a business, either large or small. Indeed all of their advice is based on experience. When we started, our Business Advisor was an ex-bank manager. In his past role, he had helped many small businesses and used his knowledge to do the same for us.

There are also the advisors who having grown their own Agency have therefore been there themselves. These people have experienced all stages of Agency growth and know the exact pathway that Agencies take.

With their experience they'll most likely be able to anticipate what is going to happen before you go through it, and so can use their highly relevant experience to guide you on how to manage your growth.

You can also use specialist Business Advisors for areas such as HR, Finance, Marketing and Sales.

The non-exec

A Non-Exec can be formally appointed at Companies House, but this is not always the case. A Non-Exec usually has a formal role and is paid for their work. They provide advice at board-style meetings.

Without question, the right type of advisor will add value to your business. When you run a business, it is easy to not see the wood from the trees however employing the right counsel can give you the clarity and accountability you need.

You will probably need different advisers at different times in the business life cycle, and it is important you do your homework before appointing anyone. It is crucial that you get two or three references, to ensure that you appoint the right person you need from day one.

Any external adviser should always add value to your company. More formally employed advisers will often offer you access to contacts and networks who will help you expand your business. So be upfront that you require them to add value and they will be worth their weight in gold.

Coach

The approach of coaches is less about telling you what to do and more about helping you discover the answer and learn for yourself. However, some owners just want to get the answers fast and may get frustrated by the coaching approach, so it's important that you fully understand what you are paying for.

It's also important to appoint advisers who have the experience of having been at both your current size of Agency, and the future size you would like your Agency to become.

What we provide when we help people through Cactus, is the ability to identify business issues quickly, combined with an understanding of what is likely to happen next in their Agency journey, and what might go wrong as well as right.

This approach can shortcut the pain of your growth journey as you won't have to make the mistakes a few times to learn from them. If you can find someone to work with you in this way it can be useful, but you have to trust each other.

Chapter 8: Outro.

CONCLUDING THOUGHTS

Agencies can be the most fun businesses of all, and often are, but they can also be very challenging businesses to manage.

After 20 years in the Agency world, we are convinced that 10% of growing an Agency is knowledge and 90% is having the right mindset.

When we sold our Agency we thought we knew everything, but our experience of Agency consulting has opened our eyes to other Agencies who were doing certain things even better.

At the time of writing, we've just passed our 10,000th hour of mentoring and consulting Agencies on their businesses.

We still learn new things every single day when working with and visiting Agencies, because of our open mindset and continual thirst for learning. We notice successful traits and share them with our clients through our training and consultancy. It helps them accelerate the success of their Agencies. Learning from best in class approaches is something you must adopt if you want to continue to evolve as all good Agencies do.

So keep an open mind, listen and learn from those people slightly ahead of you on the journey. Don't be afraid to test new ideas, particularly if you hear them from three different sources.

Jim Rohn said "Always work harder on yourself than you do in your job". We also encourage you to invest in yourself and your mental health and take regular holidays and have quality time away from the office.

Do invest time and money in personal development and learning; create the right mental framework to develop a positive growth mindset and maintain a relentless positivity that keeps you afloat when times are tough.

We also wanted to mention Leadership and make sure readers fully recognise the importance and responsibility of their role in delivering effective leadership to Agency staff.

We often find Agency leaders playing a supporting role rather than a visionary one and that's not right.

It's important, yes you support your team, but lead with your company manifesto, the mission, vision and build a strong culture with your values. Inspire and bring together your team.

Do not delegate away completely the Agency Leadership to your leadership team, remain at the helm.

Create an environment for everyone to build their careers around a trusted, autonomous, empowered workspace where a meritocratic approach to mastery is celebrated and the whole business is underscored by an authentic purpose or cause.

We hope you have found this book useful. We've shared some great follow on reading in the next section. On the many topics covered, we could have written a book on each, there's so much to say.

If you want to hear more from us or to reach out and share your Agency stories, we'd love to hear them. Please email us at hello@agencynomics.com.

Chapter 9: The Agencynomics

AGENCY METRICS, AN INTRO

Many business owners like to set staff and business targets. These are often called Key Performance Indicators (KPI) or Key Results Indicators (KRI)

The most important thing for owners to ensure, however, is that they are not just setting these targets for the sake of it.

All targets need to contribute to the company's objectives, and individual performances, otherwise your staff will get despondent at being set tasks that seem wholly irrelevant.

Any KPIs that are set, therefore, need to be defined, measurable and made evident to employees.

Benchmarking

Staff Costs/Gross Profit	58-63%	Include Directors standard dividends (where in lieu of salary), regular freelancers, Ers NI & Pensions
Revenue per head (pa)	£75,000	Across all team members
Revenue per fee earner (pa)	£120,000	Just fee earners (assumes £800 day rate at standard recovery rates) include PMs
Net profit %	9-14%	Growing Agency
Net profit %	15-25%	Agency optimised for profit
Min annual billing to recruit role	£72,000	£6k pm of one service until you recruit
Marketing budget as % of GP (to achieve high growth)	10%	Includes marketing salary & associated costs
Fame budget as % of GP	3%	
Pod Sizes	£750k-£1m	In Gross Profits

PM workload	£500,000	Minimum threshold before hiring another
AM	£800,000	Minimum threshold before hiring another
Sector concentration	25%	No one sector more than 25% of annual revenue
Deal Size % of GP	20%	No one deal more than 20% of annual revenue
Value of weighted pipeline	3 months GP min	Total Opps under 80 days x gut feel
Billable vs non billable staff	80:20	Typically this level, but can vary
Office - sq ft per person	100	Some businesses go as low as 60, if you run a call centre.
Rent as % of GP	3-6%	Depending on geography
Working Capital	85% of debtor book	Include overdraft facilities, loans advanced & free cash
Balance Sheet Net Asset Value	2 months costs	Costs = fixed overheads

Current Ratio	Minimum 2:1	Remember to split any financing between < and > one year
Sickness rate	1.5% of lower	
Staff Turnover	15% or less	This is a healthy level
Pitch win ratio (on qualified opps)	50% 33%	Under £3m turnover Over £3m turnover
Agency Business Peak	Sep-Mar Apr-Aug	60% of annual GP 40% of annual GP

Chapter 10: All leaders are readers - Jim Rohn

RECOMMENDED FURTHER READING

People are inspired by books and the ideas in them. So why not start a book club, acquire a library, get Agency Kindles or put books in your New Starter Packs!

The famous management consultant Peter Drucker spoke about a "Knowledge Organisation"; The importance of developing a culture which continues to embrace on going learning and development and will have a positive impact on a company.

Here is a list of our some of favourite books, some of which we have been mentioned/referenced, but for ease of use you can view a complete clickable list here: **http://bit.ly/Agencynomics**

Account Management:

How to Win Friends and Influence Profits - David Keane
The Art of Client Service - Robert Solomon
What Clients Really Want - Chantelle Glenville

Sales:

Pitching to Win - David Keane
Getting Naked - Patrick Lencioni
Pricing with Confidence - Reed K Holden
Give and Take - Adam Grant
How to Win Friends and Influence People – Dale Carnegie
Influence - Robert Cialdini
To Sell is Human - Daniel Pink

Networking with Millionaires - Thomas J Stanley
Reach Out - Molly Beck

Culture / Organisational structures

Maverick - Ricardo Semler
Drive - Dan Pink
Reinventing Organizations - Frederic Laloux
Delivering Happiness - Tony Hsieh
Get a Grip - Gino Wickman & Mike Paton
Traction - Gino Wickman
Holacracy - Brian Robertson

Finding purpose

What Colour is Your Parachute – Richard N. Bolles
Man's Search for Meaning – Viktor Frankl

Delegating tasks

One Minute Manager - Kenneth Blanchard

Mindset

The Magic of Thinking Big David J Schwartz
Mindset – Carol Dweck
Who Moved My Cheese – Dr Spencer Johnson

BONUS SECTION: AGENCYNOMICS TIPS

FOUR PILLARS

There are Four Pillars underpinning every Agency and these are as follows:

- Sales, Marketing & Account Management

- Financial Intelligence

- Leadership Culture and Talent

- Service Delivery

We have curated 100 of our favourite tips across these four sections to help establish best in class behaviors in your Agency.

SALES, MARKETING & ACCOUNT MANAGEMENT

1. {Lead Generation. Make a list of all the people that have ever referred you a lead, whether you won the deal or not! Now send them all a personal thank you note, small gift or arrange to take them for a drink or dinner to say thanks.}

2. {Sales. If you want to sell value not time, you must first understand how to buy value not time. Go back to all your suppliers this week and ensure you haven't selected just the cheapest, ask them how they can add value to your business.}

3. {Lead Generation. Some of the largest Agency new business wins we've come across started with a lead from a speaking event. Is your Agency doing a minimum one to two speaking events per month? Remembering that best in class Agencies do three to five speaking events per month! Why not form an Agency speaking club tomorrow?}

4. {New Business and Account Management. In a recent study of MBA students, 90% of them were able to come to successful and agreeable outcomes that were typically worth 18% more to both parties, by finding something in common with each other before negotiating. Always find several things you have personally in common with your prospects and clients.}

5. {Account Management. Manage your clients, don't let them manage you. Client service teams should not check their emails until 11am every day and use that precious time to be proactive and prepare presentations for clients, If you can't manage that for some reason, then why not create one day each week like "Future Thursday" ensuring there is one day a week dedicated to planning future ideas and activity for your clients! You owe it to them!}

6. {Aspirational Clients. Get their attention. Send a non-refundable credit note to your dream prospect for £10,000 worth of work, only on condition you can showcase the work in a case study; they'll need to meet you to brief you, so an easy way to meet them face to face.}

7. {Network Connections. If you don't ask, you don't get. Ask your local MP's Councillors, Celebrities, Influencers, that live in your area to come to an event you are organising at your offices or nearby, give her/him plenty of notice, ask them to support your local business, get a testimonial, local press, blog, you'll be amazed at how many business contacts she/he/they will have!}

8. {Lead Generation Marketing. The best times of year to be more aggressive on Marketing and especially Events are April and September.}

9. {Socialising. Super Connectors. Who are the best and most connected people in your network? Do you have a network of connectors in the sectors you want to find new connections and business in? Do you have a top 100 connections list? If not create a plan today to make a start. Reach out to someone today that can help your kick start your super connections, arrange to have a coffee or lunch with that person, do something that the future you will thank you for. Remember build genuine friendships and always seek to help others first.}

10. {Post Pitch Analysis. Losing pitches can be tough, yet it creates an exciting opportunity to learn from failing. Create a questionnaire to get some honest detailed feedback on what you did well and not so well and consider getting someone external to ask the questions. You may find the quality of feedback increases.}

11. {Pitch Win Ratios. Typically Agencies Sub £3m win 50% of qualified pitches with 33% being low and 75% excellent. Over £3m Agencies will typically win 33% of qualified pitches.}

12. {Content Strategy. Get everyone in the Agency to write a 150 word blog article on something related to marketing, creativity or tech in next 30 days then release one story a day for a month and repeat.}

13. {Prospecting. Use LinkedIn Sales Navigator to identify your top 500 prospects. Save as lead. Download the app on your phone and start to use subtle/soft social selling techniques to build trusted connections to a stage where you can invite leads to events you organise to build chemistry and demonstrate your credentials. #alwaysbeauthentic}

14. {Trade Press. Campaign, Marketing Week, The Drum, Wired. Take an hour a week over a cup of tea or coffee to flick through all the industry press for your Agency services. Keep updated on who does what and for whom. Build connections with the people writing and featuring the articles. Always share with the wider team standout stories and articles that impact your business, team and clients.}

15. {Thought Leadership. "Do not covet your ideas. Give away everything you know and more will come back to you." — Paul Arden}

16. {Awards. Another approach to Agency fame and awards is to create your own formal internal Agency awards. It's a great way to encourage and reward everybody in the team for their approach to continued learning, development and mastery of current and new skills. Get creative with other awards in areas like embracing company core values, creative and innovative ideas. What about awards for your best clients, suppliers, partners. Additionally look to reward your team for their contribution outside of work community/society/charities/causes.}

17. {Client Services. Re-Pitch to your top 10 clients annually. Take fresh ideas, treat the pitch like it's competitive, show them how much you value their business by putting in as much time in with them as hopefully you do on your new business pitches.}

18. {Agency Client. Guest Hospitality. Think about the whole end to end experience of an office visit. It's not about big budgets, just the little things attention to detail. First impressions and last impressions. Clear directions, best transport routes, where to park, what payment apps do they use? A warm greeting, a welcome choice of stunning platters of food and drinks. Suitable for the time of day. Stylish (matching unchipped plates and cups). Toilets that are clean and checked prior to visits. The best coffees and teas (not served cold or lukewarm, unless requested), healthy options, unhealthy options. Research people's favourites, remember their drinks choices. Get them their own mugs. Be creative, innovative make every guest value the experience when in your office. Think first class not cattle class!}

19. {Aspirational Client List. Take some initiative today, with a creative or marketing person from your team organise an office survey asking everyone to list their dream client. Mix in your current key prospect brands. Create a poster (or something visual) internally with all those brand logos visualised. 10-50 brands should do it. It's amazing how many times we've come across Agencies who've done this and by

the end of the year have managed to start working on one or two of their aspirational brands. This exercise helps everyone in the Agency tune into the work these brands are doing. Helps everyone be more aware of names of people at that brand who could be prospects. It also helps everyone be more aware of their connections within the Agency, who may have a way to help connect to contacts at one of the brands. You will hopefully all sub-consciously and unconsciously start to work towards connecting and working with some of those brands. If you then ever meet one of those brands you can show them they are one your Agency's dream clients. When you win one of them, always celebrate the success, it will help you believe you can win more!}

20. {Your Perfect client. What does your perfect client look like? Have you ever (or as a team) taken time to describe them in detail. If so, is it time to do this exercise again? By doing this exercise you'll start to understand what are the things you'll need to undertake to create the right environment for a "perfect client" to work with you. Sure, they'll work in the role of X and work for y type of company that's Z in size. What about one that is a relationship and value (not a price sensitive) buyer. A client who is always open to new ideas and always finds budget to help you solve their business challenges. A client who is senior enough to make decisions alone? Who will meet and speak to you regularly. A client who calls you in advance when there is a problem to give you a chance to resolve. The client who when they leave their

job they take you with them every time. Perhaps they are a fame or social client who shares common interests with you so it's easy to get on. What else? There is no question that the more a client has a personal trusted relationship, where there is strong chemistry, has shared values, that the client will on the whole be more likely to be your perfect client than not.}

21. {Existing client new business. Step 1. Pick an existing client. Imagine their business was your business, what are three things you would do to improve their approach using your Agency's services? Step 2. Create a presentation with the three ideas on it. Step 3. Book a meeting to catch up with them and share with them the three ideas. Have more than three ideas? Great share them all. Let's go big or go home here, have a quick team stand up, ask everyone for their ideas too for the client. Let's make an agenda for the whole Agency to get even more proactive with from now on!}

22. {Reciprocity. This week let's build some extra positivity for you and your Agency with this 10 day challenge. Over the next 10 days go out of your way to help at least three people per day, selflessly. For example why not write a LinkedIn recommendation each day for the next 10 days for your colleagues, clients, network contacts. Or, you could do something kind and proactive to help someone at work, or simply ask people if they need any help at all, make someone a drink, pay a compliment, buy them a small gift of appreciation. Gift them an app or a book! Tell a client how

much you appreciate their business, perhaps send them an anniversary card of working together or do something proactive to help them. If after 10 days you can see a real difference in the impact this has make it part of your daily routine.}

23. {Agency Marketing. Create ideas to make your Agency internal marketing budget stretch a little further. Perhaps aim to double your Agency's marketing budget? Work with your complimentary strategic partners to co-fund your events that way they'll cost 33 or 50% less to run. Test charging for your events for non-clients, create additional training led events and charge accordingly. Some strategic partners will even offer matching marketing incentive schemes. What about charging for your thought leadership pieces? Of course still distributing complimentary copies to prospects and clients too. Look at your annual marketing plan, get creative about how you can stretch your budget to work harder and smarter for you.}

24. {Can you answer this question without pause or hesitation. "What are you selling?"}

25. {So, who exactly, are you pitching against? https://bit.ly/2vSGjU5}

26. {Existing Clients. Isn't it about time you scheduled a "persona" workshop on your key clients. What are their

commonalities? What could you learn? How could you use the findings to improve your client experience?}

27. {Client of the Future. There is lots of talk about the Agency of the Future. What about "The Future of the Agency Client." Perhaps it's time for you to look at the 'Now, Next and Future of your clients.' Perhaps you should organise a round table breakfast with your clients as an excellent starting point for some research and thought-leadership.}

28. {Business Connections. Who are your top 100 business connections? Do you have a list, mindmap or tagged in crm? How often do you meet them? Don't have a top 100 Connections? Then start a plan to build the list.}

29. {Agency PR. Start to keep clippings of other Agency stories that appear in the trade and industry press, XX new starters this year alone, new client wins, record growth, culture related (Agency appoints nutritionist), New office/location, award wins, certification or qualification of team members. You'll quickly build up a bank of ideas, and opportunities for PR that maybe you didn't think were even newsworthy, but keep your Agency in the limelight and create a positive noise about your Agency business!}

30. {The little things. Every year for the past 12 years or so, we get this birthday card from a car finance company personally signed from David. We haven't used them for 12 years but every year we are reminded of him and his business and

have recommended him a couple of times. Imagine all your clients past and present still getting a personal card from you now for their birthday, or the day their company/they first started working with you. It's a great marketing touchpoint, that will keep returning opportunities, advocacy and referrals.}

31. {Office Tours. When prospects, clients or guests visit your office for the first time make sure you always give them a tour. If important visitors are coming then make sure everyone is in the office. Make sure that everyone can quickly access the best work you've done recently, so you can showcase those, rather than a load of blank screens! Not asking you to be inauthentic here, but the more you prepare for visitors in advance, the more impressive you will come across, and if that involves a few set pieces then so be it!}

32. {Through Leadership. One of the oldest and smartest approaches to creating thought leadership pieces for your Agency is through interviewing clients and prospective clients on a particular subject. It's a great way to find out their business challenges. Think about how by them helping you create a thought leadership report or white paper benefits them personally and professionally. 1. Helps them build their personal profile. 2. Features them in report as an expert. 3. Leads to speaking or panel opportunity at your events in future. 4. They will feature in a book perhaps. 5. You will share the results with them, which may give them further insights.}

33. {Trade Offs. When selling to new prospective clients who tell you "you've won the pitch" then proceed with now let's negotiate and talk prices, always remember to ask yourself what's the trade off here? What's the value in kind, if you have to take money off, then what are they prepared to cut out or supply you with goods or services to that value? Will they let you use their facilities for events? Let you buy their products at a discount? Talk at your events? Provide a video case study or testimonial? Let you submit their work for awards? Introduce you leads? Introduce you to their organisations partners?}

34. {Closing Opportunities. If a prospective client is trying to negotiate on the price on a piece of work, and whether your approach will to negotiate on price, add more value, or creating a value exchange, the first thing you must ALWAYS ask the client for is the day they will sign the order if you are to consider this. Always make the negotiated offer subject to a particular close date. It helps you leverage a compelling deadline and close date.}

35. {Motivation. As a good friend of ours Daryll Scott once said "Would you run faster away from a man eating tiger, or faster towards £10m pile of cash" Think about it, is it fear that drives you? Targets and goals? Or both!}

36. {Competing against bigger Agencies. Former CEO of Avenue A/Razorfish and Wunderman once said to us "any small

Agency with 10 good people can win against any big Agency, as there are never more than 10 good people in the largest Agencies he'd worked in }

37. {Account Management. Client services should aim to work in their clients offices on a regular basis. Perhaps once a month. You should know your clients organisational (within reason) chart as well as you know your own Agency one.

38. {Lead Sources. Two major size leads from mainstream car manufacturers spotted in pipelines this week. One from a squash partner, one from a social conversation about being a vegan. Once again a reminder to us all of the importance of building trust and find authentic "common" interests and connections with all the people, prospects and clients we meet.}

39. {Set Pieces. Always organise a set-piece when inviting visitors to your offices. Create an experience to remember. Start with an office tour. Where everyone knows to quickly switch to a predefined piece of work, either your best most interesting work or one highly relevant to that guest. Make all your visitors get to see the best version of your Agency at all times.}

40. {PR. Write amazing quotes for all your suppliers. Write quotes and references that they simply cannot ignore, to publish or share to all their clients. Blow them away, use superlatives, positive power words, get the quote right and

they'll put you on all their marketing materials. Offer a video testimonial. Help them to look good and they'll certainly refer you back at every occasion.}

41. {Marketing. If 80% of sales are made on the 5th to 12th contact. How are you engaging in real life with your prospects on a regular basis? Create the experiences to make that happen!}

42. {Socialising. We heard a very experienced Agency owner this week, say they built their multi million pound award winning Agency by "socialising". We at Agencynomics feel socialising is a much better and more apt description and will no longer use the word networking yay! Let the socialising begin.}

43. {Client Experience. Best in class Agencies take, or go with, their clients to the big advertising, creative, technology and marketing conferences and events. Which client did you take or go with to Cannes? Who are you taking or going with to SXSW? Think about the conferences and events where a shared experience with your client could benefit your client's business strategy.}

44. {Speaking Events. If you want more leads generated when speaking, regardless of your topic, you need to be clear of the problems you solve as an Agency. The trick is to plant that message without delivering a sales pitch. Your aim is for a good proportion of your audience to think, wow I have

that problem and this speaker and their Agency can help me fix it.}

45. {Clients. Fame clients want you to help them look good in their job. Agencies should work hard to help them. Help them enter awards for the work you do with them. Plan each piece of work to be something that could be potentially entered into an award. Help them win personal awards

·Help them win awards for mutual work
·Help them achieve internal recognition
·Praise them to their superiors
·Help them achieve success in their role
·Buy them a copy of the awards you win together"}

46. {Tim Ferris Cold Message Template. Useful for Event/Speaker invites. New Network Connections. Keep it short and don't change anything unless you are A/B Testing. Dear [So-and-So], I know you're really busy and that you get a lot of emails, so this will only take 60 seconds to read. [Here is where you say who you are: add one or two lines that establish your credibility.] [Here is where you ask your very specific question.] I totally understand if you're too busy to respond, but even a one or two line reply would really make my day. All the best, [Your Name Here]}

47. {Building social business connections. Process. 1. Pick a sector based on a case study you have or create one with pro-bono work. 2. Target key brands 50-100 3. Target key

people at those brands choose 3/4 job titles 150 -400 people. 4. Search, research and identify all events where those target people may go. 5. Research personal interests that match your or your teams. 6. Identify that sector trade press. 7. Identify that sector trade body. 8. Study all "Now Next Future" trends in tech/creative sector/design sector. 9. Identify your main competitors in this sector and their key people. Follow them. 10. Socialise to meet contacts, find speaking events, create events to invite target people. Find connections to your connections. Build sector focused thought leadership and content. Benchmark your activity levels. Appreciate, this is a two year plan to start to dominate a sector. Start today what the future will thank you for."}

48. {Account Management. Have a minimum fee – If you don't charge clients for amends, they'll have you flitting between different shades of blue for an eternity. By having a minimum fee for any changes, e.g. £250, you'll force them to think about how important it really is to "make the full stop a bit bigger." When there's a price tag attached, there's a good chance they'll decide it wasn't that important after all. And if they do want to make the change, then at least you get paid for it. Also, try and group changes together – If you have clients that send you change requests every five minutes, it's incredibly costly to make all these changes individually. You have to stop what you're doing, switch projects, make a small change and then switch back. A much better way to do it is to get your clients to send you amends all in one go. If they still send you things every five minutes,

you'll need to have the internal discipline to group all these changes together - it'll save you tons of time.}

49. {Agency business peak. Winter is coming, not, Agency business peak is typically September, October, November, January, February and March. Those six months are often a 60-40% split in terms of annual billing. You have just come out of the slowest part of the year for new business with calendar and fiscal year ends approaching, now is a great time to up the marketing and new business ante.}

50. {Sales Forecasting. Aim for a sales number that is three times your weighted pipeline (total opportunities under 80 days times gut feel) that way you should never miss a target and have a better system to plan ahead on sales. Remembering that if your monthly weighted pipeline is less than three times your monthly target you need to improve your marketing. Then if your opportunity win rate from qualified lead to decision is less than 50% you'll need to improve pitch process.}

FINANCIAL INTELLIGENCE

51. {Finance. Get an expenses app in place (e.g. ReceiptBank, Expensify, Xero) to reduce the workload of all your team (finance included). Consider Pleo (https://www.pleo.io/en/) and it's prepaid MasterCard option. A number of Apps integrate seamlessly with Xero and reduce the processing time required by your finance team.}

52. {Finance. Create a simple dashboard of key finance performance indicators (KPIs) - Five important ones: Gross Profit %, Net Profit %, Team Costs to Gross Profit %, Debtor Days, Current Ratio. Monitor them regularly. Accept that spikes do happen monthly so look at KPIs on a rolling three month basis. What are they telling you? Do you need to staff up? Are you allowing customers too long to pay their debts? Take action.}

53. {Finance. Do you have a system for credit control? This is one of the most important jobs in the business. Make sure its completed regularly by someone else (not the owners or those working on the account) and that there is a fixed process for managing cash collection. }

54. {KPI. Total Wage cost (including Director drawings) to Gross Profit should be 55-63% and 63-68% for faster growing Agencies who are investing in scaling more than 30%+ per annum. At 55% you may be stretched with not enough

people. At 70% you probably will have too many people, poor cash flow and be inefficient.}

55. {Finance: Do you offer different services but simply review one overall P&L each month? Start using Xero's tracking function to separately report on different service lines. Is that new service line really profitable? If you don't use Xero, get on it!}

56. {Finance. Always get three quotes for anything and ask the supplier to evidence what additional value they bring to you. Leverage those relationships.}

57. {Data. 55% of business leaders expect to use a small or medium sized Agency, instead of their AOR, for marketing projects in the next year. Source Globality and the Economist Intelligence Unit 2018.}

LEADERSHIP, CULTURE AND TALENT

58. {Culture. Do you have Agency core values? If so, can you recite yours by heart? Perhaps it should be a test by the end of probation everyone can? Are they memorable enough to learn? How do you honestly score, against the values? How could you improve personally by living and breathing them more visibly?}

59. {Time Management. Forget your to do list, what is this week's to don't list? What are the things you must stop doing? Prioritise what's important not what's urgent.}

60. {Vision. Start talking about your business to everyone as if you are six months ahead of where you are right now, talking where you will be, opposed to where you are now is the quickest way for you to get to that point. It creates a self-fulfilling prophecy for your vision}

61. {Learning and Development. Future proof your Agency. Become a Knowledge Agency. Encourage your colleagues to invest in their futures. Agencies today need to reinvent themselves every 18 months, with new service offerings coming into most Agencies every six-12 months. Start an Agency book club, in-house training sessions and talks. Knowledge share on trends in Slack, email and encourage you and your team to listen to Audiobooks and Podcasts. Let your team have access to Udemy, Udacity, and Lynda to access high quality, low cost online training tools!}

62. {Your team. When recruiting new team members, try where possible to determine whether candidates have a good personal network that they can potentially tap into. It doesn't just have to be their existing clients – just how well connected they are generally. Ask them how many LinkedIn connections, Twitter followers, etc they have to gauge how connected and liked they are as individuals. Whilst it won't

be a primary reason to recruit someone, it can be a very important factor in helping build business opportunities for the future.}

63. {Celebrating Success. When you get told you've won a new piece of work, don't celebrate too soon, your probability of the work actually going ahead and starting is only 95%. Our research has shown us that around one in 20 deals never proceed after a verbal yes. Once you have a signed order / contract or have received a purchase order, THEN it's time to celebrate. Always celebrate success in your Agency!}

64. {Leadership. Every Agency Leader should do a weekly team stand up, recorded for those not in the office or away to watch when they are back in.}

65. {Remember as the famous philosopher Mike Tyson said "Everybody has a plan until they get hit". What's your plan B?}

66. {Minimising Risk. Remember everyone in the Agency should help prevent "eggs in one basket" syndrome. To ensure a healthier financial and client relationship/revenue model, always work hard keep the Agency's largest clients revenue below 20% (ideally target less than 12%) or have a plan to do so! Also try to keep each sector you target to 25% of your revenue. If you focus on one sector as an Agency make sure you serve all the periphery areas to that sector.}

67. {Mindset & Mental Health: Be kind to yourself. Also be smart and more proactive with your annual leave planning. Use September as the month to plan your holiday breaks for the year ahead. Do this as early as possible. Make sure you take regular breaks at regular periods. Ensure at least 75% of your holiday/ breaks are without your work phone/social/email/messaging apps. Consider the option of using a second phone, perhaps an old phone if you can't see you not being uninterrupted. Give your main work phone to a colleague perhaps. Plan and be creative, Some of you may choose to look for the five week months where you can take two weeks off and not impact the working month too much. Book or reserve the flights or accommodation in advance to help you commit. The more regular breaks you take the more resilient and better you will deal with the challenges that #Agencylife throws at you.}

68. {Mindset. At the end of each day identify three good things that have happened that day. Reflect and then appreciate that these good things happened to you. Forget dwelling on the negatives. Focusing on the positives will help put your mind in a happier place.}

69. {Find your Inner Child. And enjoy today! Listen to music from your teens whilst you work, have a little fun. Be playful, creative, have a moment of brilliance at work and lighten up a little. Be grateful for all the things in your life! Be kind and nice to others.}

70. {Talent Management. 33% of employees knew whether they would stay with their company long-term after only their first week. Create on-boarding parties to make new starters feel welcomed into your Agency rather than just having leaving parties. Create starter packs for all new recruits. Assign a buddy for the first 30 days. What else can you do to make new starters get off to the best possible start in your Agency?}

71. {Personal Development Plans. Whatever role you have in an Agency and whether your Agency has a requirement for you to have one or not, for your own personal and professional development sake create a PDP! Start with Google, SlideShare, other people you know to find and create your best template. Once created, book a meeting with your business leader, line manager mentor or coach to present the plan and create a way to execute and deliver on it. You own it to yourself. Then share the template you create with all your colleagues and Agency owner.}

72. {Agency Inspiration. Try this. Tell yourself this every morning. Starting today. "This will be the best day of my life"}

73. {Talent Retention. Get a few of your team, who live and breathe core values, to have the final say on new starters. They are the best people to judge if candidates are a true culture fit.}

74. {Integrating Work /Life balance. Take the two to four areas accordingly (as your life has them). 1. You Time 2. Work Time. 3. Partner Time. 4. Kids Time. Score them individually. "+" For too much time, "-" for too little time and "+\-" for about right. Remember sometimes it's not the quantity of time but the quality of the time spent on the four areas. Check weekly and adjust accordingly. If "you" time is "-" it can affect all the other areas irrationally. So always remember be kind to yourself, and being a little selfish in small doses can be a good thing.}

75. {Sales. Visualise Sales Process. Sales Culture is often swept under the carpet in Agencies. Without sales and cash, there is no Agency! Let's assume for the moment that your Agency creates amazing work (or strives to) does everyone know their role in the Agency to assist with sales. We don't mean designers or developers etc picking up the phone cold calling prospects! But designers and developers can create opinions, thought leadership, write, speak, help share social media posts, invite connections to events or failing that share ideas to the client service or new business team. Everyone in the business can help on sales, from front of house to finance. Take a day to visualise and get everyone to help contribute to the sales culture plan.}

76. {Time Management. Time Poor? Some food for thought! There are 168 hours in a week . How do we find time for what matters most? Let's take off sleep seven days of eight hours, then let's say you work 12 hours a day every day of

the week (unlikely, worst case), then that's still 52 hours left a week! Break down your time at work and home, work out how you can make better use of your work and play times :-)}

77. {Success. Probably the best definition of success ever. "Success is peace of mind which is a direct result of self-satisfaction in knowing you did your best to become the best you are capable of becoming" - John Wooden}

78. {Six Words. Your most important and probably your only asset are your people in an Agency. The most important six words for retention and attraction of talent are Career, Community, Cause, Purpose, Autonomy, Mastery. Put these at the heart of your PDP.}

79. {Internal Marketing Comms. One of the best small pieces of Agency marketing we've seen recently was a small internal weekly newsletter, this could be either printed or emailed focussing on internal news, sharing information on team members, covering work achievements, personal endeavours, shared learnings, events. It created a real sense of community in the Agency. Perhaps a few of you could come together and look to create something monthly to start.}

80. {Learning from Mistakes. "If you're not making mistakes, then you're not doing anything. I'm positive that a doer makes mistakes." - John Wooden. Make sure your Agency

has a culture where people are allowed to learn by making mistakes. Just make sure everyone knows, you learn from them and please don't repeat the same one twice!}

81. {Are you lucky? When recruiting, ask the question, on a scale of one to 10 how lucky are you? Never recruit someone is says below seven. It's a question of Growth Mindset vs Fixed Mindset.}

82. {Working Groups. Rather than accepting the things in your Agency you are unhappy with, why not get a few colleagues together to form a group to fix them. Being proactive to make the workplace better in some way is an excellent way for you to add value to your role and demonstrates 'A' player work ethics.}

83. {Office Standards. Like you'd spring clean your house on a regular basis, make sure your office standards are high. We walk into Agency offices often and sometimes think what must clients and prospects think! Look around at old boxes full of crap gathering dust, paper high desks (still), cobwebs, old or little crockery, messy surfaces, coats and bags on chairs. Create more storage, have regular clear up sessions. Address the hoarders collections of crap. Set high standards. It's often hard to notice how bad things can get when you are so close to it. Bring in better recycling bins. Start today.}

84. {One Step Ahead. The best team members are "Autonomous A players" and people who demand to be left alone and

trusted to do their job. The best that we come across are always one step ahead in people's expectations with them. Whatever your role in the Agency, what does being one step ahead of what is expected from you actually look like? What does mastery of your role look like? Don't know? Don't wait to be told! Get a mentor who has done your role to help you understand what that looks like. Sometimes it's ok to accept you don't know what you don't know, but it's not acceptable to not understand or even to try to find out what great looks like for the role you do! Ask yourself every day "what would the best person in the world in your role do today?"}

85. {Aspirational values. Core values in the early days of an Agency often reflect the values of the company's founders. As the business matures these core values are refined more professionally through several different processes or exercises. Overtime you may need to look at "Aspirational Values" these are the values that you wish your Agency to accomplish in the future but currently lack. What are the potential missing values you would need everyone to embrace to drive your business forward?}

86. {Writing down, sharing and being held to account on your Agency goals is key. You become 42% more likely to achieve your goals and dreams, simply by writing them down on a regular basis. While people who wrote their goals down and then enlisted friends to help them, by sending regular progress reports succeeded closer to 75% of the time.

Source. Dr. Gail Matthews, a psychology professor at the Dominican University in California}

87. {Agency CSR. Paying it forward is good for the spirit for the Agency owner "givers" amongst you and makes commercial sense too for the matchers amongst you. A great standard for an Agency approach is to pick two charities or causes to be associated with. Choose one larger charity or cause that you can form a strategic partnership with, to mutually help each other commercially, helping to raise money whilst creating personal and business connections through the charity and their other partners. It's a mutual win-win for both the charity and the business. The second should ideally be a smaller charity or cause, with more of a meaningful connection to a personal story to a person or people that work in your Agency. A charity with a deeper more personal purpose behind it.}

88. {Inspiration. It's hot! Get the team together and go for a walk in the park, go to the beach, chill out by the pond, buy the ice creams. No one wants to be in the office sweltering and being less productive. No reason not to take the laptops and use the change of scenery and environment to inspire some new ideas. Also helps the team bond more.}

89. {Culture. Perhaps it's about time you found out who you are and what you are like. Consider getting the team to complete personality profiling and sharing the results. Help each other to grow. https://www.16personalities.com/}

90. {Hiring for a small Agency. Make a list, check it twice. What things are you doing that you want to do? What things are you doing that you never want to do? (Project Management anyone?) Your next hire probably needs to be the role that will want to do the things you don't (and if we're honest, are probably better at it as well).}

91. {People Analyser. The people Analyser is a great tool to review yourself and also your team against your businesses core values. Read more here and view the template. https://blog.eosworldwide.com/blog/95505/traction-thoughts/assessing-team-people-analyzer/ . Note, whilst EOS can suit some organisations, we are not endorsing EOS at Agencynomics, as we prefer flat structured organisations.}

SERVICE DELIVERY

92. {Project Delivery. "Give me six hours to chop down a tree and I will spend the first four sharpening the axe." — Abraham Lincoln. When starting a new project, rather than just booking it in the studio and ploughing on ahead. Get the delivery team together for a quality project kickoff meeting. Talk through at least three different ideas/ways you could deliver the project smarter and more efficiently. Investing that time up front will always pay off in the long run.}

93. {Experience Design. What's your client experience? Is it best in class? Sure you deliver them great work? But, what else? Do you help them look good in their job? How are you helping their career? How are you helping them with their peer Socialising? How are you helping your client with their knowledge development? Remember the better the client relationship the better the work, the more they will be open and trust your suggestions. Would you love your client experience, if you were a client of your Agency?}

94. {Over-Servicing and Over-Delivery. There are a few reasons for unplanned client over-servicing 1. Misquoting from the outset, 2. Over scoping the work from the outset, 3. Poor or lack of project planning/management. 4. Inefficient delivery or poor quality execution of the work. 5. Allowing the client

to scope-creep. Sometimes it's a case of all five things! Fix your processes, one step at a time.}

95. {Productivity. Here's an idea for those of you Agency people who need to create written content but struggle to do so efficiently or effectively due to distractions. How about a low cost office laptop with no internet. Just a usb slot needed for a key. Leave your phone in the office, block some time out of your diary and find a comfortable place to write with 100% focus.}

96. {Low Hanging Fruit. Remember Pareto's Law roughly 80% of the effects come from 20% of the causes. Where in your Agency is there a 20% cause that would have 80% effect if you were to fix it? For example, you may have 10 process problems on delivery, fix the two that will have biggest impact and will fix 80% of the problems.}

97. {Productivity. Take your laptop out of the office with you without the power lead and force yourself to complete set tasks before the power runs out. Parkinson's Law.}

98. {Process. Create a plan to visualise your Agency process from start to finish. Create simple versions to share in your client and prospect presentations. Name your process or delivery methodologies uniquely. Something aspirational like The Wave or Process Flow. Understand how much time, money you have invested in creating that unique process. Put a value on it. Share with prospects "We have invested

over half a million pounds in time and money over past five years on creating our world class processes and methodologies to deliver our service to you"}

99. {Time Management. Set up a timesheet code called "I have nothing to do" and encourage people to use it. Owners: Make it clear it's YOUR problem (not the team members) if the work (billable or internal) isn't there for them. Stops time dumping to client jobs, ensuring everyone has a true picture of project profitability. Also clearly shows the resource the Agency has to do the Agency Fame projects etc.}

100. {Task Management . Carrot or Stick or both? Find someone you trust financially to be your accountability partner. Transfer money to their bank account or give them cash for an amount of money that would hurt if you were to lose it. Tell them to keep the money, if you don't complete a particular task by a certain deadline.

THE END

Even if you only found just ONE useful piece of information within this book (and we hope you found a lot MORE than that) - please could you HELP us by writing an **Amazon review as a thank-you.**

We'd really appreciate it!

Please follow us on LinkedIn, Twitter & Instagram @agencynomics

Agency Founder/CEO/Shareholding Managing Director of an Agency with 3+ staff?

Join our Agency Community (free for life)
https://community.agencynomics.com

Copyright

Printed in Great Britain
by Amazon